Kirael

Volume II
The Genesis Matrix

Fred Sterling

Lightways Publishing
Honolulu, Hawaii USA

Also by
Fred Sterling

Kirael: The Great Shift

Kirael: Volume II

The Genesis Matrix

by

Fred Sterling

Published in 2001

Copyright © 2001 by Fred Sterling

Lightways Publishing

P.O. Box 27648

Honolulu, Hawaii 96827

Telephone: 1-808-945-3965

Toll-Free: 1-800-390-1886

Fax: 1-808-952-0660

Email: lightway@hula.net

Internet: www.inward.com/lightways

Cover design: Honolulu Church of Light

Cover artist: Francis Mau

Author photo: Gene Tamashiro

Kirael (Spirit)
  Kirael. Volume II, the Genesis matrix / by Fred
Sterling. -- 1st ed.
  p. cm. -- (Kirael : the great shift ; v. 2)
  LCCN: 99-076109
  ISBN: 0-9675353-0-1

  1. Creation--Miscellanea. 2. Bible. O.T. Genesis
I-XI--Miscellanea. 3. Evolution--Miscellanea.
4. Spirit writings. I. Sterling, Fred, 1946- II. Title.

BL226.K555 2001   213
                  QBI01-200252

ISBN 0-9675353-0-1   Printed in the USA

Contents

Foreword

Such is the power of our popular culture that you probably can't see the words "The Matrix" without thinking of the motion picture of the same name. Up until the release of that movie, you might have gotten any number of answers from different people if you asked, "What is the matrix?" One meaning in widely popular use sees a matrix as a gridwork of different facts or options, laid out in a way that best organizes a situation. From biology, I remember that when we get a wound, our body forms a latticework upon which the skin cells regrow, which is referred to as a matrix. In geology, it is the base material in which we find fossils, crystals, and gems embedded. An archaic use even describes a matrix as a "womb."

These definitions all share Webster's idea of "that which gives form, origin or foundation to something enclosed or embedded in it," or a support structure of some sort. "The Matrix" in the movie is described as a system of numbers, a mathematical computer program that creates the illusionary reality in which the mass of humanity finds itself trapped. In this book, Kirael, whose use of the word "matrix" predates the movie, will explain that it actually *is* all that, but is also much, much more. It is also quite different than the dramatic victimization scenario that the movie put forth which, while fictional, affected many deep inside their inner beings and began awakening them to the true nature of our mutual illusion.

You need to remember that the matrix, which is the foundation of our third-dimensional existence, is innately non-threatening and non-judgmental. It is nothing more and nothing less than a set of rules, a structure that underlies the natural laws which define life in this five-sensory, physically oriented world of limited consciousness. The matrix is merely the blueprint for this schoolhouse planet onto which we volunteered, even begged, to incarnate to advance the knowledge of our own higher selves, and thereby increase the collective wisdom of the All That Is.

In this book, as Kirael paints the picture of the true reality of the third-dimensional matrix, please don't fall into the trap of playing victim by using the matrix as an excuse for why things are so difficult in your life and messed up in the world. Just remember, *that* cop-out didn't work when you first learned about Karma either. Keep in mind that the matrix is really just the bus in which we are all riding. The important question is: Who are you letting drive the bus?

Did you give your permission for us to go in this direction by your actions...or your inactions? Have you willingly accepted most everything that has ever been told you without stopping to question its truth? Contrary to the plot of the movie, the matrix is not an evil conspiracy by machines against humans; it is a valuable tool that is allowing six billion physical Angels to forget who we really are, and experience many lifetimes of powerful lessons. The real conspiracy is that through the ages, we have allowed some of those who understood better than we how to play this game, to make the rules for us and write our history.

After you read and truly understand what Kirael is saying in this book, and in his previous book *Kirael: The Great Shift* you will be enlightened with the information you need to change your life. Knowledge is empowering; it inspires and protects you, and you will never choose to be ignorant and inactive ever again. That's like taking the red pill in the movie.

If you are anything like me, when you finally hear the truth it's only natural to initially get very angry with the people and the groups who have lied to us in the past. Clearly, some have honestly thought they had our best interests in mind, maybe just trying to prevent some group panic attack. Others plainly wanted to keep total control of wealth and power, pure and simple. Whatever the reason, in the near future all the information Kirael is sharing with us now is going to come spilling out into the open, from governments and churches and leaders we respected. It is absolutely imperative that we just forgive them and move on. When you finally hear the truth and you trust it in your heart, take that passion that you might have chosen to waste on mere anger, and instead, use it to help co-create a beautiful new reality for the highest good of all.

For now, keep living in and coping with the matrix, but always remember that you, yourself, are a wise and powerful creator: a beloved spark of the All That Is. And please don't blame the bus if you don't like the direction it is headed. Let's use this vehicle as it was intended; take the wheel together and help steer us all home.

Tom Holowach

Preface

I have received so many beautiful shares since the first book, *Kirael: The Great Shift*, was published. They are stories that touch the heart. There is the story of the mother of a dear friend who tells of suddenly awakening one night with pains in her chest. She reached for *Kirael: The Great Shift* on her bedside nightstand and placed it over her heart. To her amazement, the pains disappeared. Another woman tells of her three-year-old daughter who prefers to hug her book, rather than her teddy bear, when she feels upset.

I have learned of people who have read the book six or even seven times. At a book signing, a woman approached me with her copy of the book that was literally in tattered shape. She shared that she had read the book so many times that it had begun to fall apart. When I asked her if I could gift her with another, she kindly refused and suggested that it be given to another who might need it more.

Kirael has stated that whether he speaks with individuals in private session or to large groups of people, his vibration resonates on seven levels simultaneously. For this reason, the greatest understanding of his words comes when the book is read seven or more times. With each reading comes a new level of awareness. With each new level, the same words seem to have an entirely different impact.

This new work is deeper and more revealing than anything I have seen of Kirael's in the past. The book opens with a conceptual explanation of where the Creator began Its evolution. This challenges the reader to examine words and concepts deeper than ever before. It invites the reader to go beyond English, the language of the author, or any other language for that matter, to discover the truths. All quotes of the Bible are from the King James Version.

The editors of this work have had to keep the continuity and information flowing while maintaining Kirael's intended meaning. Often throughout the process, the challenge has been to translate into human language, ideas and realities that are beyond the Earth dimension. At times, this has been an aspiring task.

My hope is that you experience the love and healing from a Master Guide of the Seventh Dimension. To do this, you may need to pause at times and take a deep breath to gain the scope of the ideas presented here. Yet in the end, my heart knows that it will be well worth the effort. The real message is that this is truly just the beginning for humankind.

I am confident that you, the reader, will be as thrilled as I to be part of this world called Human.

"Love is the key to everything. Love is nothing more or nothing less than the Creator. When you say to someone, 'I love you,' it is the same as saying, 'I hold you in God's Light.' And when you hold one in God's Light, do you not hold one in your own light?"

—Kirael

Author's Introduction

L iving in Honolulu, with the constant "pressure" of beautiful weather and colorful rainbows can sometimes be trying, especially when the only important thing in the morning is rushing off to work. On this day, my wife and I were running late for work, and the pressure was on.

The drive to work ordinarily takes a slow thirty minutes, but on this day, traffic on the highway seemed to be moving at a different pace. As we reached the hill overlooking the city of Honolulu, it dawned on me that I was driving faster than usual. At the same time, my wife and I were in the midst of what I will refer to as a "stimulating sharing of opposing views." Our discussion held most of my attention.

When I returned my focus to the road in front of me, I suddenly saw a wall of cars with screaming red brake lights on. All the cars were at a complete standstill. All five lanes of traffic were filled with vehicles. In my mind, I immediately assessed the situation and saw that my options were non-existent. A quick glance to my left had told me there was an opening, but it was too narrow for a car. Only a motorcycle would fit in the narrow strip running alongside the center meridian.

Then in an instant, everything switched to slow motion. I could see everything vividly—the car trunks buckling and tail lights bursting. I could see the face of a little girl as she peered out the rear window of the car she was riding in. Even my car was sliding out of control in slow motion.

Time moved at a grueling pace. Helplessness took over my entire being. There was not enough time to do anything. Prayer was all that I had left, so I begged God to protect my wife, the little girl, and all the others who were in harm's way.

My car continued to slide out of control. Yards became feet. Feet became inches. Then, in a moment, something unexplainable in human terms took place.

In a last ditch effort, I veered to the left, tires screeching. Then abruptly, the sound of screeching tires disappeared. In its place was a silence that filled every part of my reality. The car seemed to be shrinking. It got smaller, even narrower, to the point where it seemed to be losing its molecular structure.

Time stood still for a split second. In that instant, we found ourselves in an alternate dimension. I looked around and saw that we were alone. There were absolutely no cars in front of us or around us. The silence was deafening.

As I frantically tried to make sense of all this, I heard the sound of my wife crying. It was a sound I had never heard before. Although it seemed to come from a distant place, it guided me back to this world. I distinctly recall reaching out my hand to comfort her. A quick look in her eyes told us both that, just moments before, we had crossed into a world outside our reality.

In those brief moments, all the colors stood out vibrantly. The world seemed to dance in brilliance. The sky appeared bluer. Even the sounds around us resonated in crystal-clear tones.

The cars began to surround us again. Abruptly, we found ourselves back in the usual stop-and-go traffic. We were safe.

My entire world shifted in those few fleeting moments. Everything in my life changed. Within days, my life took on a new perspective. I discovered that I could predict what people would do before they did it. I began to see people's auras that curiously changed with their moods. But that was just the beginning.

When I sat with people and listened to their conversations, my mind would be in two places simultaneously. Still hearing what they said, I could see them in other lifetimes as well. I knew that I was seeing things that the person speaking needed to know.

Since that day—indeed, since that life-altering experience—my connection to the world of spirit has grown stronger. What I once regarded as "airy fairy" has become more real than the illusionary world we live in. My life has shifted into a place where happiness is a daily event. I now know that everything has a purpose and that the Creator allows us to experience everything.

The work that follows will allow you to see for yourselves that reality is based on your thoughts. Matrixes are creations of thought. Levels of awareness are limitless.

Your journey of awareness, like mine, has just begun.

Kirael's Introduction

T here is an ancient Chinese proverb that says: "Give a man a fish, and he eats for a day. Teach him how to fish, and he eats for a lifetime."

Told in another way, the story goes that a man approached a fisherman and begged for a fish. The old man responded by saying, "Instead of giving you a fish and feeding you for one meal, wouldn't it be better if I showed you how to fish? In that way, you could feed yourself." The man replied that he had no interest in learning how to fish. The hunger that raged within his stomach well overpowered any desire to search for knowledge.

The same story is told in yet another fashion. It takes place along a great river where a huge tree had fallen into the rushing waters. So large was this tree that a man could walk onto it and fish for his meal. And it came to pass one day that a great sage decided to sit upon this log to collect his ration of food for the day.

After fishing for a long period of time, the sage finally caught a fair-sized fish. With great satisfaction, he placed it carefully on the log beside him. A young man, who was passing by with his wife and two children, saw this and guardedly approached the sage. He asked for the fish explaining that his family was in need of food.

The old sage happily offered to teach the man how to catch his own fish, but the sage was quickly rebuked for his offer. The man was not interested in learning a skill. He merely wanted some food.

The old sage remained fast in his resolution to offer only his teachings and sent the man on his way. All the while, he continued to fish. Soon, the sage caught another larger fish. Seeing this, the young man hurried back onto the log. He beseeched the sage to give him a fish, as there surely was more than enough for the sage.

The sage grew perplexed, wondering if it made sense to give this young man a fish. After all, he really did have more than enough.

As the sage contemplated this dilemma, a light appeared at the end of the fallen tree. At first, the greatness of this light frightened the sage for he had only heard of such manifestations in ancient stories handed down by his teachers. The light began to overwhelm him with an energy he had never before experienced. Filled with awe, the old sage heard a booming voice addressing him. The light spoke to him with such calm and beauty that the sage immediately knew he was in the presence of a great and wondrous teacher.

And the light spoke.

"Old sage, allow me to express a thought. If you choose to build upon it, it will change your life for all time to come.

"First, take from your pocket the sharpening file that you have carried with you for so long. While we speak, begin to sharpen the hook that you have tied to your line. Sharpen the hook like no other in the world. Make it so sharp that when the fish takes it in its mouth, it will feel no pain. Then, when you are ready, pray with me the following:

> *I call on the Creator to help me search out the oldest fish in the river that is ready to leave this dimension, for it has experienced all it came to experience. In that Light, guide it to my line. Knowing the fish's life plan is complete and that I have sharpened my hook so well, we join together to fulfill our journeys."*

When the light finished speaking, the sage cast his newly sharpened hook into the water. Moments later, he caught a fish of the greatest proportions. But before the old sage could begin to celebrate his newfound clarity, the light spoke again.

"If you look on the shore, you will find a string of lighter weight. If you attach your hook to this lighter string, the hook will reach deeper parts of the river. This will allow you to catch even larger fish."

The old sage did as the light suggested. His efforts were again rewarded by landing a fish ever so large. Then another fish, and yet another.

He thought this was as good as it might get, until the light offered still more guidance. The light told him to concentrate on his wrist. By flexing his wrist more when casting his line, he could send the hook out even farther.

All too soon, the pile of fish was so large that the sage felt fulfilled in his accomplishment. He set aside the fish for his meals that day. The others, he released back into the water.

Then the sage recalled the young man who had asked for a fish. He noticed that the young man was on the shore not far away. Surely, he thought, the man will ask for a fish again.

To his wonderment, he saw that the young man was busily sharpening his own hook.

The Moral

The moral, my friends, is to never teach another person something that he or she already knows on some level. Focus instead on sharpening your own hook. By perfecting the art of what you already know, you will most certainly enhance the world in your own way.

Be not the teacher, but the student. Rather than tell others what to do, focus on perfecting your own journey. In this way, you remain the consummate learner. As you do so, all those around you who seek wisdom will experience the same learning. They will be inspired to perfect their own journeys.

So concentrate solely on sharpening your own hook. Sharpen it so well that those needing the light of knowledge on their path will enter into your light. They will learn from one who chooses to learn through experience.

Apply this in your own life, and your knowingness is truly awakened.

Author's Insights:

On many occasions, Kirael has made it clear to me that he is not my teacher. Instead, he is like the sage who offers guidance to help me sharpen my hook. He guides me to find my answers. My answers are my own.

Like the young man begging for a fish, I now understand that there are no shortcuts. In order to complete any of life's lessons, they need to be experienced to the fullest. In that way, I have learned to perfect my own journey.

And that is how a fish story changed my life.

1

Creation: The Evolution of Light

Kirael's Numerology:
A "1" day is your opportunity to reconnect to the God Light within
you and to know that something completely new is about to begin.
It is interesting that this day always follows a completion day.

Author's Insights:

How many of you have asked the question, If there is a Creator, why doesn't someone explain where It all began? Or, does this all-powerful entity that humans have worshipped, and in many cases feared for so long, have an origin? Can the complexity of Its origination and existence be reduced to the written word?

As these questions arose in my mind, an explosion of lights and sounds absorbed my entire beingness. It was as though time never existed, and the whole of creation was present in one brilliant flash.

There were no third-dimensional words for my experience. I was in complete knowingness that Kirael was now willing to assist the human world to the next level of awareness. It was clear that the human world had chosen to experience the duality consciousness of this third-dimensional matrix, for as long as possible.

In order to experience this Great Shift spoken of in my first book, *Kirael: The Great Shift*, we must be willing to see the third-dimensional matrix of thought in its full reality.

It would take Kirael's energy pattern of light to help create the visions that we, the people, have a birthright to remember. It is time for all to discover the true meaning of the one word which throughout the universes has no opposite. That word is Love.

What follows is Kirael's explanation of the monumental experience I was so fortunate to experience.

Kirael Speaks:

Long before the planetary systems brought themselves into existence through the reality of focused light, there was no beginning, and there was no end. There was just the epitome of grace. The Creator, having no one to name Its energy, was simply seen as light, a self-perpetuating golden light made of what will be referred to as "light particles." So minute and free were these particles of light that they seemed to have no destined course of action. Yet once the evolutionary journey began, they would initiate the process of "all" creation. Thus, to see how the Creator began Its own journey, we will need to travel far back, beyond even the illusion of time.

Light Particles

And so it began in the purity of existence where light particles floated freely in a sea of unconscious replication. At some point, one particle joined in transition with another, and created a new spark of light energy to become known as an experience. When these two brilliant light particles touched each other, a sound emerged that sent out a wavelength of energy.

So new and exciting was this interaction that it was immediately repeated again and again through a process referred to as "evolution." Evolution simply means that when energy has experienced all that is possible to learn at its current level, it evolves to the next level of potentialities in order to experience more.

Immediately, the harmony of this experience gave birth to the possibilities of an evolutionary journey. The light particles would join together, feel, release, only to join with another. Because there were no words for this new experience, all that remained was to feel. Once it was discovered that they could experience this new sensation of feeling, they continued to attract other light particles to interact with. The possibilities seemed endless.

Each contact created a new experience that soon illuminated into new journeys. Each time light particles touched each other, it was as though they forgot for a moment that they were a part of the All That Is. It was as if they had produced a new form of life that all forms of light could interact within.

Light Particle Streams

New discoveries continued. Next, it was discovered that by vibrating at a new level, the light particles could magnetically stay attached as long as they desired. More lines or streams of particles were created. As more particle streams joined together, the grander the experience became.

These streams of particles soon began an interlocking process as one light particle stream crossed over another. As two streams of energy intersected, there was a feeling of grand beauty that went through them. They had discovered that the touching of two light particle streams created yet another level of magnetic vibration which allowed them to travel together. So they continued their journey through what seemed to be eternal space, enabling them to experience at twice the rate that was previously possible.

From a single-dimensional experience of light energy, they had moved to a world of duality. They had created many more new potentialities through this two-dimensional experience. These streams of particles now understood the complexity of combined life extensions and realized that together they would come to some form of completion.

Then it happened. A third stream of light particles crossed over the paired energy stream and the world of the Trinity was born. It was discovered that three particle streams could be held together in a vibration never before experienced. This trinity light formation would henceforth be remembered for all time as the trinity of "Truth, Trust, and Passion," and ultimately, it would become the foundation of all dimensional realities.

New discoveries and experiences that are founded on the trinity of Truth, Trust, and Passion continue to this day, but on almost inexplicable levels. I say "almost," for I have now come to your Earth plane to bring new clarity of understanding to this all-powerful essence known as the Creator. In that, we must be willing to proceed.

Trinity of Creation

The vibration in the center of this newly formed trinity reality was so intense that it began to resonate within itself. The light particles realized that by resonating one to the other, they could expand their own patterns of light energy. As their energy amplified within the center, it would move outward to the edges of the new trinity form. In the desire to experience itself, it chose to simply fold its energy back onto itself.

Through this process of light energy replicating back upon itself, the new trinity experienced the splendor of its own luminosity, the first understanding of Love. Thus, in its love for itself, the trinity light began to amplify and evolve into a process that created itself over and over again, magnetizing every particle being that existed.

So highly vibrating in brilliance was the light that it would continuously create particle streams in trinities that would also evolve inwardly within themselves until its own conception was amassed into a great energy pattern of light, a life force of cumulative self-perpetuating energy, and in that "will" was born.

This life force, having formed a will, was nothing more or nothing less than a conceptual energy of conglomerate thought-patterns of love. The life force began to understand, in its own existence, that it was in fact the replication of all life forces. In this state of awareness, it was inherently the passion needed to sustain love. In essence, this evolution of light was the origination of thought and the very beginning of all creations.

When this creation force would think of an experience, the thought would vibrate into energetic-sustaining illusions of perceived realities. By drawing on its endless supply of particles, it could take any thought and magnetically energize it into any possible thought manifestation. Thereafter, the source of this evolutionary light process with no opposing force would be known throughout all universes as "The Creator." The Creator is an energy force of light beyond gender; therefore, we would be accurate to use the word "It" in referring to the Creator.

All that you currently understand of your modern human history is patterned after what has just been shared. Each mass of particle light trinities begins life as a light particle being, which in turn becomes the life force of all living energy that would exist in any reality. Your DNA, for example, is a simple formation of particle streams. Your molecular body is a composite of particle reality. In truth, your whole existence is held in a single particle being. That is, until it invokes its energy into the world of choice, or as better stated, until it "takes a journey."

Can you see it, my friends? This all-powerful essence of light that had created all existence through the momentum of thought became aware at one point that It could experience more of Itself on any imaginable level. Levels of thought that the Creator had heretofore only imagined could now be experienced in a vibrational form of particle light illusion. One might imagine the Creator's exhilaration in the realization that whatever It sustained as thought became a reality.

Keep in mind that, at this vibration, no time existed. The span or length of space this journey took had no measure. The Creator discovered that by expanding Its own energy through trinity light formations, the capability of dividing Itself into multiple existences was only a thought away. From this, the Creator could experience an endless joy. No limitations existed, and the only thing needed was desire. Thus began the creation of life on a multitude of planetary systems.

Remember clearly that without the particles of the Creator's energy, nothing existed. Be aware that all living essence on all dimensions was brought to life in the pulsation of light particles vibrating on a sonic level created from thought.

The Levels of Light-Reality Dimensions

It came to pass that with all this creation moving at will, the Creator, in Its consciousness of all light particles, chose to define Itself in a space of measured reality that would become known as Transitional Illusionary Material Evolving, or T.I.M.E. With this new illusionary conception, the Creator allowed for the measure of Its own evolution.

Through Its own will, the Creator allowed as part of Its own evolution, a series of levels which seemingly held different dimensions that could be experienced. These levels are created as illusionary to delineate the evolution of light. Yet, they entitle all light beings to experience all that ever will be, or the All That Is.

The Levels of Light-Reality Dimensions best described by the human word would be delineated as follows:

God Creator – The omnipresence of all light particles. The God Creator presence is entirely of evolutionary vibration. The Creator's

Light unfolds by amassing reproductive light presence while allowing for fulfillment through the experiences of many journeys. In other words, the God Creator allows Its own particle light the journey of experiencing illusionary separation, while holding all truth in divinity. Every aspect of Its beingness is focused on the creation of life forms. In the completeness of love (love having no opposite), this force is the collective consciousness of the All That Is.

Light Particles – The magnetically-charged essence which forms the beginning stages of all evolutionary journeys. In order for a living energy to exist, it is made up of a conglomerate of these particles.

Light Particle Beings – The trinity formations of light particle streams that contain a vibration of love as its center core of reality. It is this essence of love that willingly encounters the illusion of separation, thereby honoring its Creator by experiencing the journey of evolution. All life forms are a direct vibration of this level. As each light being begins the journey of evolution, it never forgets its connection to the All That Is. Upon the completion of each incarnation into physical energy, the light being knows it will return to the All That Is to share the experiences of its latest journey.

Guidance Reality – Where I, Kirael, am from. Here you find light beings of spiraled vibration that have experienced all possible formations of life. They are destined to be of service to all realities on their evolutionary journeys. Those spiritual essences that do choose to be of service are often looked upon as Masters because they must have full awareness of all that vibrates on all levels, higher and lower. With the exception of designated "spiritual essences," this level of consciousness seldom interacts with the human world.

Angelic Reality – The energy patterns that vibrate closest to the world known as human. Often these beings are delegated to serve the evolutionary dimensions and intercede at certain levels of learning when necessary. In this reality, the range of angels extends from those which work closely with humans all the way to those at the Seraphim level, where they act solely at the discretion of the God Creator.

Galactic Reality – Seen by some as existing between the angel and human realities. These energy patterns have evolutionary lesson plans which range from levels that vibrate on planets which are not as advanced as the Earth beings to systems capable of transcending time and space. Those capable of transcending time and space will likely interact with the human world during the Great Shift. Those who have evolved to a complete understanding of their emotions are able to appreciate the levels that Earth beings have attained.

Humans – Aspects, or vibrational patterns of magnetic energy, designated by the higher, spirit self to experience the fullness of the five-sensory illusion of planet Earth. Upon the determination that life will manifest in a physical form, a light particle being enters the conceiving life force. At that point, the physical body becomes the vehicle used by the higher self to fulfill its particular evolutionary life plan. It is by choice that these aspects of the higher self are veiled from fully experiencing their sixth sense in order to abide with the illusionary factors of this journey called human life.

Guardians of Developmental Societies

At a certain point, the Creator discovered that it had amassed every possible experience through Its limitless travels of all dimensional realities. In this process, the Creator became full of Its own knowingness and knew that what was needed next to express Its own light were the "guardians." Hence, the Creator brought forth these energy patterns of light for the purpose of initiating the development of societies in keeping with the Its evolutionary plan.

In simplicity, my friends, you find the Creator's essence of Truth, Trust, and Passion formed within the Guardians of Developmental Societies, otherwise known as G.O.D.S. We might need to make a distinction here: The ultimate reality of existence of the All That Is is the one God Creator, whereas these G.O.D.S. are formed by the Creator and are found throughout the history of human and other developing societies.

The Guardians of Developmental Societies soon realized that a multitude of spaces was needed for the Creator to resonate to the illusion of multiple experiences. Accordingly, these light emissaries of the Creator went forth into different planetary systems which would have the potential of existing for billions of years. They sought out systems that allowed for a multiplicity of re-populations, where an evolving energy pattern could experience many reincarnations within the design of the All That Is.

Councils of Light

Soon it would become evident in the great wisdom of the Creator that a reduction of energy would be necessary to fully reveal the myriad of overall potentialities. Hence, it was determined that "Councils of Light," representing the G.O.D.S. in reduced energy forms, would be established as the best way to exist in all realities. In this manner, all could continue to maintain a force in alignment with the Creator of the All That Is.

In Its desire to keep things as simple as possible, the Creator knew It had to amplify Its energy into realities that allowed for spontaneous momentum. Therefore, the Creator chose to allow four sets of Thought-Light Particle Being trinities to form one single pattern of energy, to be known as a Council. Four such sets would then create a council of twelve entities, thereby setting the standard for all councils that followed.

Throughout the illusion of time and space, you will see that those who have attained legitimate life experiences, or societies that have reached the final stages of evolution, are self-governed by such councils. The word "governed" will likely ruffle the energy of those who resist any form of control, so let it be understood that this is a form of guidance, as opposed to a form of leadership. In fact, one should remember that the greatest desire of any council being or member was to replace itself as soon as possible, thereby offering another the experience of guidance.

Unlike structured power systems that truly desire to maintain hierarchy, the Councils of Light were to serve only by offering guidance; there was no desire to control. In this way, they attained a complete understanding of the meaning of brothers and sisters of Creator Light.

Even today, Light Council energies must maintain a complete and comprehensive connection to all realities of evolutionary worlds. They must have knowledge of love's existence within the All That Is. Love is the energy that exists in all realities.

It cannot be said enough: Even within the human illusion of duality, love has no opposite. Love just "Is."

All council decision-making is cumulative of love energy. Simply stated, only when love is the solution will a council render a proposal or some form of guidance. In all cases, however, all are allowed to follow or not to follow the guidance of a given council. It is their intention never to interrupt a lesson plan but only to offer possibilities.

Such measures continue to be strictly adhered to until today.

Evolutionary Mother Earth

Literally billions of planetary systems were developing throughout the multiple universes under the same beginnings of a revolving nebula of light particles. Your scientists describe the beginnings of your planet Earth as a swirling gaseous mass of dust, moving closer and closer together. This continued until its own evolving motion, referred to as gravitational force, held it together at its center. However, this gaseous mass was not dust. Rather, as with all other living energy, it was the phenomenon of light particles amassing. They were light particles formatting themselves into a vibrational pattern of magnetic energy, thereby giving themselves strength to establish the reality of the Earth plane.

Unlike many other planets, Earth was a planet chosen to sustain evolutionary life. Other planets in this particular system would be used throughout time to experiment with different types of life, but Earth was to be held forth as evolutionary. In this, all that had been learned from other planetary systems was brought into focused light. In the creation of Earth—with its flowing green fields, with its mountains that reached into the skies, and rainbows so full of color—was found beauty beyond expression. On planet Earth, all had the potential to be experienced in evolutionary growth.

The question quickly arises: If this awesome Creator is also the creation of the All That Is, how could It still desire to experience? The answer is simple, my friends. If you will, follow me for a moment:

Imagine yourself in the form of a light energy or spirit being, and you have before you in physical form a glass filled with the finest available wine. As you gaze upon this wine from the world of spirit, you can comprehend it only in its light pattern formation, nothing more. This would be the extent of your experience. In order to be able to touch the smoothness of the glass, or to smell the bouquet of its essence, or even to allow it to wash over the palate of your mouth, you would need a physical body. To experience the wine in its fullness, you would need the sensations of your five senses, beginning with touch, taste, and smell.

So once again, the Creator utilized the one power that had brought all this to reality: the power of thinking, or thought. Each thought held the possibility of creating enough magnetic energy to amass particle value in order to manifest its thought into the illusion of reality. In Its own light, the Creator amassed energy, whereby it could, through the power of thought, create all energy into potential lesson plans. The only thing remaining was to create a part of Itself which could vibrate at a level of understanding capable of experiencing such a reality. It needed only to honor the total experience and imagine Itself being separated from Its own light by thought alone.

The Human Experience

The Creator attempted to populate this schoolhouse called Earth with a perfect being, capable of love. It created beings that could savor the illusion of a limited reality defined by the five senses as well as experience multiple incarnations. For this purpose, the physical human was manifested into being by bringing light particle vibrations to a slower rate. In this form, the Creator, through Its higher selves, could choose life after life to experience Itself in the many different realities that thought would allow.

For example, once the Creator chose a particle of Its own light force to experience a multiple-life journey, It would begin to manifest Its energy as a light particle being. This being was allowed to enter alternate dimensions and experiences through the newly discovered formation of love, the trinity light formation. Within the illusion of separation from the Creator, the light being would vibrate down to the physical plane of Earth where the completeness of its journey was defined by how many lessons were fully learned before the physical body wore out and returned to the light to be revitalized. Its connection to the Creator was maintained through its higher self. The total intention was to seek out all possibilities and to experience every potentiality that thought could provoke.

Upon arrival on the Earth plane, a light particle being in human physical form begins its journey at the simplest vibrations of learning levels. It needs to experience what most people reading this book would see as "lower life" situations. For instance, if one wishes to experience what holding up a small store felt like, it is likely to be a younger soul who is just beginning the journey of experiencing the All That Is.

As the soul evolves or ages through incarnation after incarnation, and as lessons are learned, it no longer needs the low-vibrating lessons. Thus, the soul chooses not to play in that arena any further.

Humans would be kinder to each other if they understood that in any situation, they are simply witnessing a fellow soul searching to experience each option at every level. Therefore, before you judge the next person doing something you regard as "bad," remember that at some point in your own evolution in one lifetime or another, you too have likely sought to experience a similar situation.

Thus, by permitting Its energy to be present in all beings, the Creator experiences each and every moment of Its creation. A single particle of this great Creator essence is all that is necessary to start the journey of evolution. After each lifetime, the light particle being returns to the Creator to share its experiences with all living forces. Then it honors its Creator by willfully returning to Earth to gain more experience.

Here is an important message to all evolving light particle beings of the Creator: Please remember that no matter which level you are vibrating in at this moment, a golden thread of light keeps you in alignment with all levels that are returning to the Creator.

At this point, the old adage reminding us that we are all brothers and sisters in one human family can take on a different light. You may choose different colors of skin and shapes of eyes, but the truth is, we all come from the same light. The Creator is the all-encompassing energy of existence. The Creator does not sit in judgment of Its own beingness. Through the human experience, the Creator simply desires to gain more to Itself. Finally, when all becomes clear that the All That Is was created in the simplest form of thought, all will see the simplicity of the Creator's plan.

Thus, the master plan unfolds.

Questions and Answers

Q: How does one explain the Creator of the All That Is in simple terms?

Kirael: The Creator is the epitome of the All That Is, and defines Its reality through thought.

One needs simply to be capable of understanding focused vibration of magnetically-charged thought personification to see that light particles are the essence of the All That Is. The interesting thing, my friend, is the energy that sustains all reality in all forms is actually quite easy to explain.

Using third-dimensional words to describe the Creator, one simply must allow for a power which has no limits—a power that desires to experience all possible variations of vibrations, while allowing for the total being of all realities in all forms. Once the Creator makes the collective decision to create in definable terms, It simultaneously commits to experience each creation. Through thought patterns, the Creator renders thoughts, best suited to experience Its own creations, all in the name of self-love.

The Creator allows the living essence of each to enter into illusionary journeys in order to ultimately know enlightenment. In Its infinite wisdom, the Creator chooses to separate into countless illusionary possibilities, thereby increasing all levels of possible experiences It has brought to life through thought.

This all-powerful source sits not in judgment of Its individual expressions such as you. The Creator simply allows for the existence of illusionary time to let Its individual expressions completely learn all aspects of awareness on whatever levels of creation.

Q: If the All That Is began in the simplest form of thought, where did that thought come from?

Kirael: In the beginning, light particles simply allowed all experience to be of pure ecstasy. When it came to pass that one could join to the next, that experience needed to be defined. Words did not exist at the time, so it became necessary to create evolutionary journeys. In this way, multiple experiences began to unfold, and it became necessary to place them into some kind of order. Today, we see that as thought.

It can be clearly established that a single thought is the derivative of multiple outcomes. In this wondrous illusion of possibilities, thoughts may appear endless, and each choice gives way to a new and fuller journey. Be not confused as to where thought comes from, only understand that without it, there is no beginning and there is no ending.

Q: Is the Creator God the Ultimate Creator, or are there higher levels of Creators than what we are capable of conceiving?

Kirael: There is only one Creator within all the galaxies. Understand that in this one galaxy alone, you have over 200 billion suns with planets circling about them, suns just like the one you can see with the human eye. If your imagination is vivid enough, focus on the thought of two hundred billion galaxies just like this one, and you will begin to get a glimpse of reality!

In all invocations of life, there is only one source of light, and it all began as creation. When you understand that all comes from the Source, the journey to comprehend the Creator begins. It may be described in many formats, and it is likely that each description will differ in varying vibrations of awareness. Yet the ultimate vibrations of the Creator are in totality the omnipresence of all evolving realities.

Once the particles began to evolve, a new collective awareness was formed within this new energy pattern. In that, a new journey became its own creation. It collectively began its procession, and the Creator became aware of Its own light.

Beyond this reality, no additional power is manifest, for in Its own light, the Creator is the All That Is. As a rule, planetary systems that are seemingly apart from the world that you inhabit do not refer to the omnipresence of God as "God" or as the "Creator." This is because long ago they accepted that they are part of the All That Is and have no reason to distinguish any separation. These systems understand that their life force is the journey of this "omni" life force of collective alignment, so they understand love.

Q: Is the Creator of Itself evolutionary?

Kirael: It might be better said that the Creator *is* evolution. In the constant pursuit of the experience, all light evolves to the understanding of knowing. Because the Creator is of the same light and is in constant motion, It too continues to perfect Its illusion of the experience, as long as love is maintained as the focus. In Its omnipresence, the Creator experiences the awareness of newer perspectives and continues to endeavor to allow each that is awakening the availability to reformat existence in its own illusion. By so doing, evolution creates evolution, and light is never ending.

Q: Was it the Creator's consciousness that created the planetary systems? If so, were there other forces or light entities involved? How did the light particles that created planetary systems know that they were supposed to do this?

Kirael: My friend, the word "creator" is another form of the word "creation." There is nothing that exists that is not of the Creator's force of energy. Because the questions about this omni-force are aligned to human verbiage, we on the Guidance level have to fit our answers into the best layer of words that hopefully enable you to come to a conclusion best suited to your own growth.

Prefaced in such a manner, I will attempt to answer this query by reminding each of you that in your self-imposed and limited view of the whole, you see your planet as a hierarchy of destined particle lights. In fact, your entire matrix is the culmination of generated thought, which serves as a schoolhouse for your five-sensory expression.

It so came about that the Creator brought forth different systems of awareness, one of which was a planetary system to evolve magnetically-charged life forms. In Its quest to experience as many full realities imaginable, the thought sequencing used by the Creator to create focused life was for the purpose of allowing different vibrational lives to exist, each sustaining varying systems of sound and light pattern creations. This explains why so many different forms of systems were thought into existence. Your planetary system, my friends, is just one of the myriad variations of vibration allowed for in the All That Is.

Q: It feels good not to have to fear the Creator, so how can I get others to see this as well?

Kirael: The truth is that it isn't important to sway another's belief system. Instead, it would be more important if each one became so absorbed in the focusing of their own thoughts to an advanced level of awareness that all around would then see the great rewards of evolution. This would be enough to make the other seeker yearn for more.

When the Trust of the trinity of Truth, Trust, and Passion develops deeply within, one is then okay with everyone else's beliefs. When a person is so deeply immersed in the Passion of learning his or her own lessons, he or she naturally attracts energy of the same light vibration. All that remains then is raising oneself to a new and higher level of vibration.

Be clear on this: A soul just beginning the many journeys at lower levels of vibrating essence will be experiencing many lessons that you have already encountered to varying degrees. Remember that your light and theirs are on the same journey, just at different levels of awareness.

Q: When I call upon the I AM Presence in my meditations, am I calling upon the Guardians of Developmental Societies, or the particle streams that created those Guardians?

Kirael: When you call on the I AM Presence, you are attempting to create communication into the spirit or higher self.

Let me explain this by continuing my discussion of the Creator's process of creating. As the Creator defined Its energy by amassing Itself in different levels of vibration, It was clear that different vibrations of embodiment would be necessary. Each level of vibration was dependent on how densely the Creator would need to reduce Its energy in order to meet the needed amount or severity of each level.

In the case of humanoid awareness (from which humans today originated), there is a minimum of two levels used to reduce the Creator Light within each aspect. The first level is referred to as the oversoul, and this is the existence of a multitude of differing awarenesses combined in the preservation of a thought system. This is then reduced by the illusion of separation into higher self realities, which are finally vibrated down to magnetic patterns of illusionary body processes (each individual human being).

Most higher selves allow a trinity of aspects or energy patterns from the oversoul to venture into a human reality, thereby enhancing the higher self's ability to experience on multiple levels. As a rule, the three aspects are separated by such vast distances that the likelihood of stumbling onto each other's path is almost non-existent.

At the time of the shift from this Third Dimension into the Fourth Light, or Fourth Dimension, the human aspect that has attained the highest level of awareness will receive and utilize the light force of its other aspects. In its collective force, it will establish itself in the new light awareness. Thus, the more each aspect heals levels of understanding, the higher the remaining ones ultimately arrive in the Fourth Light.

Q: How would you describe the world of Guidance?

Kirael: This, my friend, has as many answers as are conceivable in your thoughts.

A very simple answer would be that the Guidance level is where one finds a mesmerizing conglomeration of sounds and lights without the physical thought manifestations found in this dimension.

In a recent "Evening with Kirael" session, I was asked to describe how the Guidance level of awareness looked. This is how I responded: First, you would need to draw a visual representation of thought vibrations of the most extra-sensory possibilities. Then you would have to multiply that by a million. What you see would be only the most limited exposure into a world that exists solely in particle light.

In the world of Guidance, or Masters, meaning those having completed all levels of four-body vibrations, it is time that only when the worlds are ready for great shifts in consciousness do we fully integrate our light into a particular planetary system. This was the case when Jesus chose to walk on this level of awareness. He clearly knew that it was time for humans to move to the next level, and in his love for humanity, Jesus fulfilled one of the greatest incarnations ever recorded. Still to this day, the teachings of Jesus are the one understanding that could carry the enlightenment of your world into another world beyond your current matrix.

Thus, we of the Guidance world are now readily interacting with your world so that this time around, the Great Shift can be experienced without having to bring life to an appearance of closure. This Great Shift is being done by the human world through a One Consciousness of Spirit. Those who are willing to expand their light to new levels of understanding will experience the most powerful awakening this planet has ever allowed. As you approach the Fourth Dimension and begin to comprehend the magnitude of new possibilities, only then will you realize the miracle of life!

Q: What is your relationship with the Creator?

Kirael: When I am not in state with the medium, I am in what we call "natural state." In order to be in state with the medium, I must realign my light vibration to the vibration of the matrix within which the human world exists. I am literally a focus of light particles reflecting the Creator's desire to advance evolutionary societies.

My friend, each formation of life is a result of vibrational light patterns designed with one purpose. No matter what level of consciousness each formation of life is vibrating at, it is a total expression of love. If creation is the culmination of developing awareness, then the intent of each presumed aspect of energy is to recreate the full being of light in harmony with the All That Is, and to that I am no exception.

The intention of my light is to communicate to the different vibrational patterns of light that are in perpetual motion, the evolutionary stage that each has attained. I simply monitor all levels of awareness in the name of Creation. And it is only at times of great shifts in wakefulness that I enter my experiential light into the physical world.

Q: What are the effects on my own light particle body when I meditate and prana breathe regularly?

Kirael: The entire physical body system is based on conceptual alignment of sound. Each of you is made up of a complex system of light vibration, and you need only harmonically allow for cellular cohesion to exist in the matrix of thought. In doing so, you allow each cell to vibrate in attunement with the full awareness of the whole. When you begin to relax the entire vibrational awareness, each cell of your body becomes attentive of the existence of harmony in each and every other cell. In this harmony, a collective focus becomes the primary vibration, and your possibilities of healing go into motion on a multitude of levels.

In a meditative state, the cells are brought to a level of vibration where they allow for the harmonic resonance to remember their connection to the All That Is. In that space, they are not controlled by the matrix thought system. Thus, healing and understanding take place on the highest level.

In the art of prana breathing, you are simply allowing for the particle light of the highest value to compensate for the erosion of the inner consciousness of each cell. When the illusionary body system is infused with golden light, or prana, the capping ends of the DNA on all fully vibrating strands are re-absorbed in its highest remembrance of perfection. Thus, the more you allow the infusion of light into the densely vibrating physical system, the more you understand the awakening possibilities of the Great Shift.

2

Duality: The Journey Begins

Kirael's Numerology:
A "2" day reminds you to be aware that yin/yang situations are all
around you. On this day, it is best to take a look at where your life is,
and to move your thoughts into a higher trinity level of understanding.

Author's Insights:

The Bible has served lifetimes of individuals, and it seems that as an evolutionary energy, each time the human raises its level of awareness, this great work becomes clearer in understanding. There are many that maintain this work holds the same meanings today as the day it was written. It would be well to remember that as the Bible was brought to life, the men responsible for it most likely viewed the Earth as being flat, and that if you journeyed to the horizon, you would fall off the Earth. With this in mind, let us explore the possibilities of the writings within the Bible.

For the beginner, the Bible often creates more questions than answers when viewed in its entirety. This is because the Bible is a map of evolution for humankind to follow. Many questions may arise while studying this map, but you may be secure in the knowledge that if followed, you are allowed to conclude the reality of your own heart. If it is so that we are all of the Creator's essence, then we will each know the truths that exist in the Bible for each of us, and we will never be threatened by another's interpretation.

I invite you, the reader, to remember that you are a child of the Creator. So when reading a passage from the Bible, allow your knowingness to interpret the meaning behind the words. Those who tell you to accept each word literally are likely not ready for change, and I say here, change is all that remains.

Kirael Speaks:

Approximately 1,700 years ago, the core essence of the Bible as we know it today was scattered among a multitude of written documents. Some records were documented on parchment, and some on weathered scrolls. Others were simply stored in the memory of those who were selected to eventually put them in written form.

After a time, it seemed necessary to condense the assortment of all these documents into an easily readable manuscript. This process was left up to a group of a chosen few, later known as the Council of Nicaea, who were to gather the texts into one book. The result of this would become the collective teachings of the human world. Let it be known that many important records were not added to the final version of the Bible because their contents were found to be potentially controversial to the church. These documents that were intentionally left out of the Bible were transcribed with meticulous clarity and are being held in safe keeping, some deep within the archives like those of the Vatican. The truth behind these words will be revealed only at the time of the Shift.

The Council of Nicaea knew they were entering a period of great difficulty. They understood that if the Bible was worded properly, this new work could be used to govern the thinking of the people. When the final version of the Bible, the King James' version, was completed, the ritualistic leaders of the time met and confirmed its merit, for they had clearly seen that the Bible could be used to their advantage.

If we look at the original writers of the various records that would finally form the Bible, we would see that they were the first to make their own interpretations, and this groundwork would take literally hundreds of years to clear. In the end, the Council of Nicaea would, in turn, produce the Bible in a manner that best suited them.

Nevertheless, it must still remain truth that the words in the Bible are written in such a way that you, the reader, are left to your own interpretation. The multiplicity of accounts in the Bible is overwhelming, but it always comes to this: When you read the Bible, you will discover that some things feel right, some don't. Partially this is because the people have been admonished for centuries to hold each word as it is written in a very literal sense. So may I remind you that your higher self is connected into the Creator's Light, and through this connection, you will know which parts are truth and which parts have been enhanced to portray events in such a manner as to establish issues of control.

To amplify the possibilities of how one might read this great work called the Bible, please read the following verse in which the word "fear" is used.

> Leviticus 25:17: *Therefore you shall not oppress one another, but you shall fear your God; for I am the Lord your God.*

If you replaced Webster's Dictionary's first definition of the word "fear," 1) anxiety caused by real or possible danger, with the second definition, 2) awe, reverence, what a change it makes! When you look throughout the Bible and replace the word "fear" with *"revere,"* not only are you allowed to behold the Creator's presence in the highest regard, but you are able to behold the Creator without fear. If one word can change an outcome so drastically, then might it stand to reason that there are other words that may fit this same possibility?

You will soon find that much of what was deliberately left out of your Bible would literally change the way the Earth is perceived today. Much of the current-day teachings of the Bible focus on the emanation of fear, rather than on what Jesus spoke of in bringing peace to humanity without fear. In his last hours, Jesus tried to show the world that in order to create a space of evolution, all must see each other in the same light they had emerged from—the Light and Love of the Creator.

Let us now go beyond the written records, beyond the theories of the origins of human life, beyond the theories of Darwinism, to a greater possibility of truth with a more thorough explanation of the genesis of human history as written in the Bible.

Re-view of the Beginning

It is stated in the Bible that the Creator brought forth an essence in direct proportion to Its own energy. This energy would operate on one hundred percent of its all-knowingness and would be known as the spirit or higher self. It would remember that it was of the same light as the Creator. The higher self would always know it could never be separated from its own light.

> Genesis 1:26: *And God said, "Let us make man in our image, after our likeness."*

Thus, a light essence was formed that was an exact replica of God's own spiritual light. This light energy had no persona or embodiment of its own, for no separation existed between the God Light and this newly formed energy. It was in spirit form, yet it had its own defined essence. Although vibrating on a slightly different level than God, this light energy would guide the newly forming planet called Earth.

The "Particle-ization" of Atom and Evolution

As the Creator and Its newly created energy, the higher self, looked over the magnificent illusion of Earth, the Creator felt another stirring of Its vibration manifested in the form of questions. "How was all this beauty to be experienced? If all this had been brought into being by thought energy, then could not this same energy be vibrated to an even denser level where the five senses could be experienced?"

> Genesis 2:7: *And the Lord God formed man of the dust of the ground, and breathed into his nostrils the breath of life; and man became a living soul.*

Through the energy of thought, the God Creator had brought forth the formation of the first being with the intent to experience the evolutionary journey on this physical plane known as Earth. The Creator had proceeded to gather a multitude of light particles that already existed in the spirit energy of this new level. They were light particles that displayed energetic motion or "e-motion," thus making them evolutionary. And from this, man was formed.

In the Creator's desire to experience all It had created, It had brought forth in Its own light an aspect of Itself that we shall call Truth. From this Truth, the Creator proceeded to magnetically charge these light particles until they formed the atom, the building blocks of mass.

As the Creator held the thought of similar vibrations which already existed in far-off universes, it came to pass that human was vibrated into being. These magnetically-charged particles emitted a beautiful array of colorful illusions, hence the name "hue-man." So this first human, who in time came to be known as Adam (atom), began his own form of life in mass particle light.

In the simplicity of thought, the Creator had brought forth a new source of being through emotion. This new being would journey through creation, experiencing levels in the Earth dimension not possible within the spirit world. Within Adam was a great desire to experience with an even greater desire to evolve. For inherent in the human evolutionary experience was the opportunity to return once again to the Creator Light particle essence after having experienced all there was to enjoy as a human being.

Adam first experienced his own light partially in spirit form, although he began to gather the density of mass in haste. As he walked about the great garden he named Eden, he looked upon it in all its magnificence. He began to realize the vast opportunities for his enjoyment and experience. Though still not in his fully solid physical form, Adam quickly used his newfound abilities to reach out and collect a berry. First, he plucked it from its stem. Then he put it in his mouth, and for the first time, experienced the sweetness of the berry. What joy!

Yet, there was still no formal understanding of what was taking place, and Adam discovered that his thoughts needed identifiers. He understood that he would have to put everything that existed in his reality into words. So Adam began to identify each experience, each thought, by a word. He then placed each word into the system called the brain, where it became stored memory.

The Creator saw that Adam needed to connect and communicate with living energies of similar awareness. Another human companion could double the opportunities of awakening and aid in the word-building of this new society.

> Genesis 2:21-22: *And the Lord God caused a deep sleep to fall on Adam, and he slept: and He took one of his ribs, and closed up the flesh instead thereof; And the rib, which the Lord God had taken from man, made he a woman, and brought her unto the man.*

Indeed, the Creator allowed Adam to enter into a deep state of awareness. In Its knowingness, the Creator extracted an energy vibration from Adam's emotional light body. From this, the Creator formed a beautiful energy of matter that was capable of experiencing the same journey. Hence, the Creator breathed into this creation the essence of Trust, and the world of the "womb-man" was brought into being. Known as Eve (evolution), this new form would be needed for the evolutionary journey of the entire human world.

Adam and Eve looked upon each other and realized that they had been brought forth in different physical reality forms, one male and the other female. Immediately, they began to question one another, "What is it that makes you as you are, and I as I am? Yet, we as we are?" The questions that flowed between them seemed endless, and they knew that it would take an eternity to discover all the beauty of sharing their light.

As the journey of Adam and Eve unfolded, they found themselves surrounded in a glorious accumulation of tangible experiences. They found they could communicate with the Creator at will. All that they wished to experience was placed before them by the Creator in such a way that by fully understanding the process, it became a reality.

Everything Adam and Eve could possibly desire was theirs to manifest, simply through thought. Adorned with a magical sixth sense, they had only to think the thought, and it became a reality. The sixth sense, when they chose to activate it, allowed them to arrive quickly at the completion of each lesson plan. At the same time, never were they allowed to manifest a reality without it being a part of the journey because the experience was truly what it was all about.

The Light Source

Always intrigued by this brilliant, fully activated "Light Source" (likened to a tree of knowledge) that was found in the center of their Eden world, it was Adam who first questioned God of its origin. In response, the wondrous energy of the Creator became emphatic in Its desire to communicate that there was no need to create shortcuts in the evolutionary journey of the human existence. "What good would it do to create all this illusion, this matrix, and then not be able to fully experience it? What was the value of the evolutionary journey without the willingness to experience everything to the fullest of possibilities?" were the thoughts of the Creator as communicated to Adam.

Meanwhile, Eve listened to God and Adam in communion. She listened as God explained to Adam that this Light Source was the source of the All That Is and that it bore the fruits of all-knowingness.

> Genesis 2:17: *But of the tree of the knowledge of good and evil, thou shalt not eat of it: for in the day that thou eatest thereof thou shalt surely die.*

The Creator explained that if ever Adam or Eve entered into this Light, or if they decided to partake of this energy in any way, they would become instantaneously and fully enlightened. This meant that the journey of evolution would be lost forever. At that moment, Adam and Eve vowed that they would never enter this divine space. They agreed that they would never touch the Light (likened to an apple).

Adam being predominantly male energy with the need to conquer, found doing the complete journey an exciting way to experience life. Eve, on the other hand, was not quite sure that everything within a lesson plan on the journey of experience had to be completed in its totality. In her fullness of trust in the Creator, Eve believed that the Creator would care for them in all their needs. She pondered this question, and a coiled pattern of thought (likened to a snake) energy entered into her consciousness.

> Genesis 3:4-5: *And the serpent said unto the woman, "Ye shall not surely die: For God doth know that in the day ye eat thereof, then your eyes shall be opened, and ye shall be as gods, knowing good and evil."*

This coiled, or spiraled pattern of evolution, persuaded Eve into thinking that she could still attain full enlightenment of the Creator Light, even if she chose to forego the lesson plan in its fullest.

Eve was tempted, as are humans of current time who would rather attain instant full enlightenment than experience every detail of the lesson plan. And the possibility of the first spiral or repetitive lesson plan was formed.

> Genesis 3:6: *And when the woman saw that the tree was good for food, and that it was pleasant to the eyes, and a tree to be desired to make one wise, she took of the fruit thereof, and did eat, and gave unto her husband with her; and he did eat.*

The temptation of enlightenment without doing the journey became overpowering for Eve. This Light, so brilliant, so warm and inviting, was too much for her to resist.

Eve reached within, and immediately, an explosion of lights and sounds assimilated into thought patterns that she somehow understood in multi-linear thought. Imagine the turmoil she must have felt as she became aware of glorious patterns of light that she had never before experienced in her short time on this new planet.

Eve saw within that Light all dimensional realities simultaneously, and in clear, minute detail. Colors, sparkling lights and sounds never before experienced swirled through her thought process. She saw her own life within the All That Is. She recognized evolutionary life on many different planetary systems, some advanced and others that seemed to her quite uncivilized. Effortlessly, she perceived the future as she would experience it.

"Instant Ascension" or "The Journey"

Immediately, Eve felt the Creator's presence beside her, bidding her to remove her energy from this space of light particles. The Creator made it known to her that if she stayed immersed within that Light, all hope of experiencing the journey of the Earth matrix would be lost for all eternity.

Following the Creator's bidding, Eve began to focus her energy back into the third-dimensional illusion. Then her eyes beheld Adam, who was about to follow her lead. But before she could explain to him what the Creator had just shown her, Adam entered his hand into the Light. Instantaneously, he also found himself within the lights, colors, and sounds of the forbidden Light. As Adam was about to immerse himself completely into the Light, he found that something from afar was attempting to gain his attention. As his vision became focused, he found himself looking deeply into the eyes of Eve. So deep and intense was her gaze that the first experience of human passion came to be. In that moment between Adam and Eve, the trinity of Truth (Adam), Trust (Eve), and Passion (Love) was born.

In that same instant, Eve recalled what she had just moments before learned from the Creator. She knew that she would have to bring Adam back to the evolutionary journey. What Eve and Adam had just discovered—the essence of human love—would be, for all time to come, the thread to bind all human existence with their Creator. And she guided Adam to remove himself from the Light.

The Veil of Ego

> Genesis 3:8: *And they heard the voice of the Lord God walking in the garden in the cool of the day: and Adam*

*and his wife hid themselves from the presence of the
Lord God amongst the trees of the garden.*

Adam and Eve were immediately aware that they had gone against
the Creator's covenant. Realizing they had in some way become
separated from this all-powerful essence, God, they felt certain that
grave consequences awaited them, and they began to project thoughts
that they hoped would hide them from their Creator.

Feeling the thoughts of separation projected by Adam and Eve,
God saw an opportunity for humans to veil their light. In this manner,
Adam and Eve could then pretend separation from their Creator. This
illusionary separation would thereby allow for the unfolding of the
human journey in its purest form.

Then the Creator spoke to Adam and Eve in a voice as strong as
they had ever experienced, although the voice now seemed to come
from a great distance. They heard the Creator explain that the Third
Dimension of Mother Earth had been created solely for experiencing
the journey of evolution. But by reaching into the Light when they did,
they had crossed the mystical lines of dimensional realities.

Within the Light Source, Adam and Eve had found themselves in
lights and beauty of color and sound beyond the Third Dimension. As
a result, they would find the density of the third-dimensional
schoolhouse impossible to tolerate. Therefore, if the human experience
of evolution were to continue to its fullest on Mother Earth, the Creator
explained that a veil was needed. The veil, which could also be called
the process of Enshrouding of the Genetic Origination (E.G.O.), would
be a defined space between the illusionary limitations of the Third
Dimension and the reality of the All That Is.

Genesis 3:21-22: *Unto Adam also and to his wife did
the Lord God make coats of skins, and clothed them.*

As a self-imposed limitation, the ego-veil would allow the human
species to separate themselves from the all-knowing reality. Humans
would no longer operate at 100% brain capacity, but at a limited 10%
usage as defined by their five senses. With a more limited brain usage,
humans could learn on a level more conducive to evolution on this
planet Earth. In essence, they would no longer remember the totality of
the human species that Adam and Eve had experienced, but would only
be mindful of a limited duality existence.

With the veil process, the Creator set apart a space where it would appear that not all was known. This space would then be filled with experiences from journeys of learned lessons. By so doing, humans would be afforded the honor of experiencing each lesson plan from its inception, through the total journey, on to completion. How many lifetimes this would take was of no concern to the Creator. For in the truth of life, time is but an illusion.

Thus, Adam and Eve were reborn. From this understanding, they began to learn anew. It would be a new beginning but, without access to the total knowledge they had brought with them from the Light.

Each experience of Adam and Eve was placed in the 10% portion of their brain. Each time they experienced something new, they would use this ten-percent file system to relate it to what they had already learned. Thus, human memory was established. It is for this reason that humans today continue to use information already known to attempt to solve situations of new lessons not yet experienced.

The ego-veil would also act as a protector from the temptation to jump ahead in any lesson plan without doing the complete journey. The Creator wanted the human world to journey without shortcuts, which often the human world would see as punishment. Yet, in truth, there was then, and still is today, no other way to truly experience the totality of this grand schoolhouse called Earth.

Hence, in a moment's span, Adam and Eve began to forget. They began to lose sight of the truth that they were one with the Creator Light. The ego, the Creator's shield of the illusion of separation, was in place. The trinity force, formed of Truth, Trust, and Passion, made humans willing to suspend their knowledge of the All That Is. Ultimately, this opened the way for all humanity that followed to experience the journey called evolution.

The Illusion of Separation

Thus, begins a new human journey as a particle of the God Light not separated from the God Creator, except in the 10% brain thought.

> Genesis 3:23: *Therefore the Lord God sent him from the Garden of Eden, to till the ground from whence he was taken.*

Simply, Adam and Eve were allowed to forget their experience even though they felt they had been banished from the only world they knew. Yet, in the wisdom of the Creator, it was only by self-limiting their knowingness could evolution unfold.

If evolution were to have any credence, the Creator saw that humans would have to be shrouded in the illusion of duality, or opposites. If humans were able to use their full power of recollection and could recognize that they were of the same energy as their Creator, then there would be no reason to choose to experience evolution. For this evolutionary understanding called "human" to do the journey and experience every possible lesson, it would have to be willing to at least pretend separation.

Another element was still missing, however. In order to make the illusion of separation complete, fear was needed. Thus, the Creator allowed fear to be born: the fear of possibly never again remembering the oneness with their Creator essence. Can you imaging one day knowing the full existence of the Creator, and the next day experiencing a dimmed recollection of the Creator and not feeling the fullness of the Creator's love?

This fear has prevailed at one level or another within humans throughout the entire span of the Third Dimension. The fear of loss or separation energized by the ego has given humans a greater experience of the illusion of separation. Yet, this fear of separation has made them strive harder to once again become one with their Creator.

It is through the remembrance of love that each chooses to evolve. It is through love that each becomes an integral part of this totality. Hence, my friends, the beauty of your ego has allowed each of you to experience the journey of evolution back to the All That Is.

The journey called "Life" began with Adam and Eve bringing forth the Light from the essence of the Creator. From this Light, the experience of all humanity would grow. In allowing each the experience to evolve, the Creator had set the stage for the lesson plans to be learned at a pace that would always encourage the return to the fullness of Light.

Spiraling Through the Multiplicity of Lives

The Creator decided that the journey of human evolution would be bestowed upon a select group of spirit energies. It would be granted to all those willing to be perceived in the luminous light particles that form the human energy pattern. Of greater significance, however, was that the journey of evolution would only be allowed to those who were willing to create as many experiences as needed to reach a full remembrance of the illusion of separation.

Therefore, one after another of the spirit world would approach the Creator offering to be of service—a service that each understood would send their light force reeling into the world of spiraling lesson plans. These spirit beings, held in the fullness of the Creator's Light, would allow their presence to be vibrated to a physical human presence. In so doing, they would be able to experience all that the Creator had thought into existence. As humans, they would touch, taste, smell, see, and hear all the beauty that existed on the Earth plane.

These soul energies knew that the human journey might require a multiplicity of lifetimes to complete. This condition was accepted as these souls were honored to do the will of the Creator. Starting with the simplest of life plans, they would work their way through the complexities, only to discover that the journey was uncomplicated all along.

As each soul aged through its incarnations, it would ever so slowly begin to discover that it had never left the Creator's Light. It had only perceived such to be. As each soul aged, by returning again and again to the Third Dimension, it would often have to repeat lessons not learned through repetitive experiences. Yet, by choosing to incarnate lifetime after lifetime, the lesson would eventually be fully understood, only to move to another new and exciting level of experiences.

Angelic Observers

While all this was taking place, my friends, the Angelic Realm was watching with great regard. They had approached the God Creator and asked, "When will it be our place to be of service to the human journey?"

The Creator had responded by directing them not to intercede in the human world, unless the request was initiated from the human level. In addition, the requests of humans had to be clearly impassioned before angels could intervene, for the Creator knew that an abundance of intervention would quickly reveal to those on the human journey that no real separation existed between the two levels.

The Creator spoke again.

"One day we will send our spokesperson and they will

listen. Until that time, I ask that you of the Angelic Realm simply listen to their prayers. It will take the humans many, many centuries to learn to pray in Truth, Trust, and Passion. When they finally do learn, that is the sign for you of the Angelic Realm to interact with their illusion.

And so it shall be known that before the Great Shift comes onto their world, they shall open the path for you to enter, and you shall walk beside them. For the most part, they will not know that you of the angel world are there, for still the grandness of their ego system allows them to feel cut off from all other levels of love. Stay close, my friends of the angel world, for soon, yes soon, they will know."

Now is the time for you to know of the angels, my human friends. I ask this very moment that you reach before you, and you will come to know your own personal angels. Simply reach out your hand a few inches, and you will feel their presence. You will touch the heart energy of your angels, and they in turn will place within your heart a message of love. Yes, they rejoice in your awakening.

As we approach this Great Shift, the veils begin to diminish in order to reach new levels of thought. You must be willing to journey into the 90% human experience that moves beyond the limitations of the five senses. You must be open to experience love on new levels. The only other way would be for you to return home and watch the Shift from afar.

For you who have been led to read this work, you have earned the right to see this Great Shift through. Do not give up. Please know that you have no reason to leave. You have only reason to stay and to participate in the most wondrous, the most beautiful span of time since the actual bringing of life form to this planet.

Questions and Answers

Q: Eve was asked by God not to enter into the Light in the Garden of Eden. So why are we now being guided to enter into that Light?

Kirael: One can only imagine the power and courage it must have taken Eve to see all the multi-dimensional possibilities, yet still be willing to allow the veil of limitation to prevail. In her fully balanced love, she chose to let all who followed know the honor of experiencing all five human senses, while holding the truth that no one is ever really separated from the Creator's Light.

We are never separated from this Light, my friends; we only perceive it to be that way. Soon all will see through the illusion and will begin new, fuller journeys using more DNA strands and a much higher percentage of the brain spectrum.

As you come to this process called the Shift and move from the Third Dimension into the Fourth Dimension, you no longer need the lesson plans that you were born into. Now you will experience a reality that shifts into what your angels and guides have been trying to communicate to you.

The glory of this beautiful female called Eve, who actually allowed this to take place in the name of Creation, will be remembered as the most influential being of current history. Because of the courage of this first couple, Adam and Eve, each of you now stands on the brink of moving into the most thrilling experience known to humankind, the Great Shift.

Q: Was Eve leading humankind into their own evolutionary spiritual growth?

Kirael: Adam was created in the wholeness of the four-body system. When Eve was created, the energy to complete the female world was pulled from Adam's emotional body. All realities viewing this process stated that it would be Eve, Adam's female counterpart, who would lead humanity back to evolution. She would do this based upon the emotional energy that had been pulled from Adam.

Adam's all-powerful search for the need to explore and conquer began when he realized that by giving a portion of his energy for the creation of Eve, he was no longer complete. Hence, Adam's exploration of the world that lay before him was accompanied by the need to fill his emotional essence, as well as to understand the power of the female energy.

Q: In the spirit world, is our choice to return to the Earth plane

as humans the same as Eve's choice to withdraw from the Light?

Kirael: If one were to look at it in its most simple form, yes. By choosing to utilize a veil, we enter a world that offers a form of evolution. Yet as you leave the world of spirit and enter the illusionary energy of Earth, you are born with a full remembrance of the totality. It is said that each child is born in its full 100% knowing. Then, soon after birth, the ego begins to shadow our truth, and we begin the journey of evolution. When you chose to come into the Earth plane, you expressed the desire to experience life based within the five senses.

Q: We are all being challenged in many ways. What can we do to have more heart-strength and faith?

Kirael: Most importantly, one must remember that we have come, to a space and time called the Shift. This is where the Earth humans will begin to raise their vibrations into the reality of higher consciousness. Most who are reading a work of this magnitude have already accepted the fact that change must take place, and in that light, know that all these journeys leading to this point must now be collectively nurtured.

Humans have spent life after life incarnate to experience the complete journey of each possibility. Now that the time approaches for each to remember his or her truth, the heart is the only real way to understand these changes. The strength you speak of will come by immersing the self into the worlds of meditation, sleep-state programming, and by forming mastermind groups of lightworkers, all the tools I discussed in the first book, *Kirael: The Great Shift*. The world must now be seen through the eyes of the Creator. Know that the time to move at a quickened pace is at hand.

As we seek light and the ability to move into a higher vibration, let it be said in this fashion:

As we enter into this space called the Shift and move from the Third Dimension into the Fourth Dimension, it becomes clearer that each individual is a light particle body. That which is of magnetic structure is beginning to lose its vibrational power here in this world. In essence, many of you are experiencing the physical effects of the changing vibrational energies that are taking place at an almost alarming rate. Remember that "space in time" is illusionary, and in its own reality, has no existence. Hence, one creates the necessary lesson plans to completely understand the fullness of the experience.

The light that emanates from within each person shall resonate to the Light put forth by the Creator. As we become brighter and brighter, the ego system becomes dimmer and dimmer. In the human world the ego system is becoming dimmer in its own loving light, and all that has been the focus of fear for centuries is diminishing at a rapid rate. Our light is becoming stronger and brighter as we increase our own understanding of evolution. More and more, we are in the God Creator's Light and moving into a higher value stream of knowing. Through this Light, ascension begins, and our ability to see one another as brothers and sisters comes to a higher reality.

3

Trinity: The Matrix Unveiled

Kirael's Numerology:
On a "3" day, be guided by the trinity of Truth, Trust, and Passion.
Feel it create a new essence of love awakening about you. Some-
thing bright and beautiful is about to take place in your life.

Author's Insights:

The entire world we live in is an accumulation of thought process. This means that everything that we see came together through thought. Every thought you and I have becomes part of the collective thought reality, or matrix. Therefore, a matrix can be defined as a culmination of thought.

Perhaps it is better to first see how a matrix is established, as in the case of the Earth matrix. In this way, we will hopefully find answers to questions that some are now asking. For example, How did we arrive at the point where we fell into accepting everything "just the way it is"? Where was the matrix pattern established? Was the matrix system so well masked in the beginning that even the wisest often overlooked it?

Then there are those who ask about "doom and gloom." They want to know, How bad is it going to get? Or, Is there a secret government? The answers to these questions, and more, will unfold as the matrix is exposed. For now, I can say that not only is there a secret government, but that "we, the people" are part of it. It is not unusual to find the human race looking to blame some outside force for their woes, while pretending that "we, the people" are helplessly being swept along. This has worked in the third-dimensional reality, but as we move to new and higher "in-lighted" ways of evolution, we, the people must be ready to move to the next level of understanding.

For this reason, I have asked Kirael to encapsulate the most significant parts of human history into one chapter, focusing on how the matrix of Earth was created. In this chapter, Kirael offers a new historical interpretation of human evolution. It is the divine plan of the Creator that with this new understanding, each of us will gain the awareness to complete all third-dimensional lessons.

The Creator has designated this current lifetime as the "clean-up" life for those who are in human incarnation to experience previously missed lessons. This may account for the extremely full lives we are working through at this time. This may also account for an almost constant feeling of stress in the lives of many. Each of us on a cellular level understands that this is the last time we will be able to experience many of our duality-based realities. With Shift energies rapidly increasing, it is clearly evident that the Creator will hold the veils of illusion tightly in place, thereby offering humans a way to heal all past issues.

Just when you think you have finally found the key to life, a new chapter takes you to another beginning. The work simply continues to begin.

Kirael Speaks:

Mother Earth has had innumerable inhabitants on her planet over millions of years. Each time the life force of this planet was diminished, the possibility of new life was born. In the past, ice ages and other cataclysmic upheavals have been vitally important to the evolution of Mother Earth. During these periods, her inhabitants have vibrated to different life forms. Some have gone into hibernation, not of the physical body, but of the light particle essence. The life form of that period would relinquish its physical vibrational form and return to its light particle essence. That essence would remain in the etheric fabric until the atmospheric realignment made their reformatting possible.

In some extreme cases, small pockets of humans actually went to live underground while waiting for the disruptive energies on the surface to pass. Many were direct descendants of the Lemurian society who had learned not to succumb to fear. Instead, they learned the true meaning of the Creator's love.

The one constant population throughout the history of Earth has been the whale population. They have been the only mammals of evolutionary capacity that were able to survive the ice ages. In even the most challenging of times, these creatures have persevered in much the same form as we see them today. History has been handed down lifetime after lifetime within their massive brains. Hence, the whales have become known as the "record-keepers" of the planet. When the time comes for the whales to communicate more directly with humans, the knowledge they reveal will provide the basis for rewriting Mother Earth's entire history.

At this point, it must be made clear that in all stages of evolution of this planet, the Creator has remained ever-present in some form or another. The Creator has never given up on planet Earth. It certainly has no intention to do so now as the Earth shifts into the next evolutionary stage, the Fourth Dimension.

In the Beginning...This Time Around

Your scientists will show through measurable data that the last time Mother Earth endured expansive ice masses covering her surface was 30,000 to 40,000 years ago. As the Earth began to thaw towards the end of the Ice Age, land masses were once again pushed to the surface by moving ice and were readied for life. Ascension began anew with the reintroduction of the plant world and a life-sustaining atmosphere. The natural progression of the animal kingdom then followed, which collectively set the stage for the latest incarnation of the human species.

As with any other re-population of human magnetic existence on Earth, the Creator was willing to start at the beginning and to simply observe as evolution progressed. The key was that the particle light within each human was kept aware of its previous incarnations. From that point, new journeys would unfold.

Because of the human tendency to rush from one learning experience to another, much had been missed in previous incarnations. Thus, the Creator would "de-evolve" or regress human life to the very beginning. It would then evolve it again through every possibility, seeing to it that nothing was left out. Thus, every single lesson that had not been fully experienced in previous lifetimes could be played out to the fullest in lifetimes to come.

This current human incarnation began on the shores of the water world. Water, being the embodiment of spirit, enhances all life forms in the beginning stages of development. Thus, each human incarnation onto the Earth plane began in liquid. Each would be spiritually amassed, whether it be the sperm and the egg of liquid form, or the liquid in the mother's womb.

In the infinite wisdom of the Creator, life is given the ultimate assurance of survival by dispersing itself in all possibilities of existence. Hence, as life began to amass in human form, it would literally be scattered around the planet through the vibration of particles. The humans would "a-light" in places simultaneously. No one place held a higher truth than another place. Life was to be spread to the far reaches of this planet, and would be weakened into extinction, or strengthened into a thriving force, by the physical elements of the planet.

The golden light particles amassing into human form near the equator, or the "common center," flourished in the beginning. With food and water resources available in abundant and constant supply at the equator, humans could let the forces of nature guide their existence. Life prospered in the easiest possible manner with little or no need for tools or shelter.

Humans were exposed to the sun on a constant basis, so the Creator aligned the particle value of the human skin to simultaneously absorb and reflect the sun's rays. The more one was exposed to the direct rays of the sun, the more skin reflectors were amassed to create a darker shade of skin pigmentation. Those of darker skin at the equator would initially develop a stronger spiritual connection to the Creator. During this period of history, love was re-established between Mother Earth and her inhabitants.

The Journey "From" Never Ends

As the populations along the equator flourished, the humans were forced to search for fresh water. They followed the clouds to the mountains and beyond. Rather than return to their points of origination, they chose to create new living spaces in far-distant regions. Where previously sleeping under the stars or simple shelters had been sufficient, humans found the need for more sophisticated shelters. Most significantly, by moving greater distances from the sun's full force, humans began to lose some of the reflectors in their skin, thereby taking on lighter shades of color.

Man's constant search for fresh water led to human migration at both points north and south of the equator. It also led to greater challenges for human survival, all within the Creator's plan to enhance human existence. For example, when ice shelves began to melt at higher elevations, animal populations were forced to move to lower elevations. This increased the possibility of their coming into contact with humans.

Humans who ventured into uncharted areas would encounter animals that were capable of outsmarting the humans and their crude hunting implements. Those humans who chose to hone their hunting skills were rewarded with the bounty of clothing and materials from these animals.

Learning through the challenge of each new experience was becoming an exciting way of life. Humans were finding that meeting the test of each encounter with success was the greatest challenge. Along with that came an intense desire to move into other unknown territories.

It wouldn't be long before the inner senses of the humans would give them reason to challenge the greatest of obstacles—the water itself. Prior to that, when humans first came to a great expanse of water, they walked for hundreds of miles to find a crossing, or spent a lifetime seeking a solution to this obstacle.

It happened one day that a tree fell across a river, giving the humans access to the other side. Then on another day, the fallen tree floated down the waterway. Humans found that they could travel to new destinations at great speed by holding on tightly to the tree branches. As this form of transportation evolved, the raising of wind catchers on the floating crafts and the bright lights of the night sky began to unveil whole new worlds to experience. No longer held captive by foot travel, the early explorers continued to discover ever larger, more bountiful lands by moving beyond their self-imposed limitations of fear.

Those choosing to remain in one place built a future where domesticating the animal world for food and clothing led to the cultivation of vegetation and controlled waterways. In their ever growing need to feel that they were in control of a piece of Mother Earth, humans strove for higher and higher technology. Henceforth, size, strength, and cooperation became the challenge, if not the plight, of the human world.

The Formation of Power

At a given point in evolution, a new breed of humans appeared, who were significantly larger than the average person. This stronger and more powerful being became known as a larger giant. Over a period of time, this larger giant dominated the area it inhabited and a hierarchy based on physical size was established.

For example, in the gathering of food on a tree covered with ripe, luscious fruits, the average human could reach only the fruits on the lower branches of the tree. He was forced to leave the best fruits at the top because they were beyond his reach. So it became necessary for the smaller human to ask for help from the larger giant to harvest the upper bounties of the fruit trees. Soon, the larger giants realized that their stature could be used to utmost advantage over those with less size and strength. Conversely, the smaller ones found themselves much too dependent on the larger beings. The smaller humans were compelled to offer gifts to the larger giants to maintain their services and keep them in their midst. Hence, the larger giant came to be luxuriously cared for by the masses of smaller humans, all without having to put forth much energy. All seemed in perfect harmony, until the mind overtook the heart.

In due time, the larger giant became complacent in his role and the same time, insisted on greater and greater bounty for the usual services requested of him. The bounty became so large that the smaller humans needed to amass their resources to fulfill the larger giant's request. Thus, the world of barter was born, which, in turn, amplified the thought consciousness of greed.

The larger giant's demands continued to be filled until the smaller human discovered that he could mount his domesticated animals and by its speed counter the larger giant's strength. If the smaller human picked up a large stick and rode very fast, he could overpower the larger giant and be gone with the collected bounty before the larger giant could even contemplate striking back.

Then the smaller humans came up with an idea. They thought, what if the number was multiplied? Mounted on fast-moving horses, a number of them could band together, plan their attack, and easily overpower the larger giant to gain their bounty. With such cunning, humans attacked fellow humans for their bounty as well. All too soon, the amassing of wealth was conceived, and this new way of life became a major force that would guide humankind through the entire third-dimensional journey known as the matrix experience.

Thought Overpowers Emotion

These new bands of roving marauders created a hierarchy by electing one responsible to plan the next strategic moment. By everyone supporting the one who was the fastest thinker, the others could centralize their efforts into a swift-moving marauding force. They proceeded to amass great riches with ease. Thus, the world of mastermind was born—wherein collective thoughts and efforts were sustained to achieve a master plan.

You will note that the first use of masterminds was for the purpose of establishing and enforcing control over people. Next, it was used to establish dominions of physical space. Those of a mastermind group would strategically place their people in designated places as observers, thereby establishing dominion. One could only learn of the mastermind's power when someone was seen as out of alignment. The wrath of this unseen power fell upon the unfortunate person.

The unseen power had grown into an exploiting force that was faceless and nameless. All the more reason for the common people to be fearful. Those tending the fields or caring for the animals dared not question this new power, for in truth, no one knew where to find it. It became clear to this invisible force that fear, real or imagined, was all that was needed to keep the masses subject to its control. Does this sound similar to today's "secret government"?

Meanwhile, the most clever of them appointed himself as leader and accepted all the bounty received on behalf of all the bands of roving marauders. The leader kept the absolute best of the bounty for himself. He divided the remaining with the others, according to their strengths. Hence, a social order was born.

Next, the marauders sought out the most highly traveled trade routes along which the largest rewards could be found. They soon concluded that they no longer needed to travel long distances to gather great riches if they built a fortress along a heavily traveled part of the trade route. In that way, the riches literally came to them. They needed only wait for the treasures to cross their path.

The evolution of power seemed endless. At first, only a margin of the wares coming before them was demanded as payment for crossing their path. But as time passed, the marauders demanded more and more goods, and more and more riches of the travelers. Soon, travelers also found taxes imposed upon them in exchange for wares and services.

Then the building of structures began in earnest. Fortresses with great walled structures were built. Empires within the fortress walls were established. An empire needed an emperor, one who would prove to be the shrewdest amongst his fellow ravaging marauders. The emperor was the most able at convincing his cohorts of maintaining the masses under control through fear.

The emperor often utilized a mythical monster, such as a fire-breathing dragon, to threaten a commoner into yielding to his power. The threat was simple: Obey the laws established by the emperor, and he would restrain this horrible beast from reigning terror upon the commoner. The threat of mystical monsters over the people began to lose its effectiveness when the emperor was challenged to prove their existence. So, the emperor needed to find something or someone that he could put before the people to again instill fear.

As the emperor walked through his empire one day, it came to his attention that a certain individual was being treated differently by the people. He was viewed as strange by some and held in fear by others. This person had an uncanny way of knowing something before it would happen, or used some new, magical powers to heal someone. No one questioned the source of those powers, and the emperor saw his opportunity.

A deal was quickly struck. In exchange for residing within the fortress walls to do the bidding of the emperor, the one with supernatural powers was treated royally by the emperor's court. To the masses, he would be known as the mystic, or spiritual advisor, to the emperor.

In this manner, fear of the emperor was reinstated. The emperor could wield his power over the people with an even greater threat by replacing the dragon with the mystic. If the emperor's wrath was provoked, he claimed the mystic would cast deadly spells on the culprit.

All the while, the people were being drawn into fearing powers unseen. A secret society was being established which neither the emperor, nor the mystic/spiritual advisor, saw unfolding.

Who Is Truly in Power?

The emperor had begun in earnest to threaten the masses into doing his will. He had firmly established fear as the basis for his rule. He had also empowered the influence of the mystic/spiritual advisor. Unfortunately, the mystic/spiritual advisor had virtually nothing to do to occupy his time, so he began to travel beyond the walls of the empire in search of new adventures.

The further the mystic/spiritual advisor traveled, the more he discovered. He visited new lands rich with bounty never before seen. He met individuals of vastly different experiences who were willing to share what they knew with him. And each time the mystic/spiritual advisor went on a journey of discovery, he collected great fortunes of goods and knowledge that he shared with the emperor upon his return.

The emperor believed that the sources of his riches were inexhaustible, and he sent the mystic/spiritual advisor on more distant journeys. What he did not realize, however, was that the mystic was keeping for himself not only the vast portion of the bounty, but a great portion of the knowledge he had gained as well. This, my friends, was the true power: the knowledge that was being amassed.

As the mystic/spiritual advisor evolved to become an explorer, he met others like himself, who were also on fact-finding, treasure-amassing missions for their emperors. Together, they decided to form a pact wherein they would not share the secrets of their mystical powers beyond themselves—for all time to come. In that, they became the all-powerful entities of secrecy.

Meanwhile...Back at Home

Thanks to the newfound wealth provided him by his mystic/spiritual advisor, the emperor lived very comfortably. He always encouraged his mystic/spiritual advisor to travel in search of bigger, more exciting bounty, with no regard for where it came from, or by what means it arrived in his empire. Moreover, the emperor cared only for displaying his most recent objects of wealth to the commoners. In this way, his power was rarely questioned.

The figurehead, or emperor, was so fully satisfied with his life of opulence that he was willing to relinquish knowing the source of the riches. Instead, it was the mystic who held the power, for he knew where he could find more of whatever was needed to control the masses.

Thus, it was the mystic that became all-powerful, without any outward display of force to the people. And conveniently, it was the emperor who had to face the wrath of the people if something went wrong. All the while, the mystics continued their travels to far-off places.

Each time the mystic/spiritual advisor/explorer encountered another of their kind, they would reaffirm their agreement to withhold from their emperors the majority of their knowledge. Like their predecessors, the roving marauders turned emperors and rulers, the mystics/spiritual advisors understood that by banding together and withholding information, they could maintain control.

Their journeys were secretly recorded and the information held tightly within their group. They knew that the written document was their key to success. On higher levels of awareness, the mystics also knew they needed only to state the limited truth. Then, their abilities to garner the wealth of the Earth would be further guaranteed.

The Written Word is Presumed History

Time took on a life of its own. The recording of the past was the only way to remember where all had come from. Given that the majority of the riches came through the travels of their mystics/explorers, the emperors appointed them to keep their records. Hence, the mystics, turned spiritual advisors of emperors, turned explorers, also became the emperors' appointed scribes.

At this point, the mystics collectively knew that their power over the emperors had to be protected at all costs. The delicate balance had to be maintained between the emperors who were thought to be in power and the mystics who truly were.

So what did they do? Being mystics, they used their mystical powers. In this manner, the mystics understood that they could commune with the unseen forces of light by using an almost unheard of sense—the sixth sense. Through this sense, the mystics understood that there was no need to keep records of the past. Instead, by being fully present in the Now they would intuitively accomplish the greatest of awakenings. Most importantly, with regards to their roles as scribes, they discovered that those who were guided by the past were destined to be subservient to the will of the record keepers.

With this in mind, the mystics/scribes created two formats of recording. One format was to document the records of the time on parchment. The other was to place their records in an etheric level of awareness. The danger of the second was that if anyone from the emperor down to the masses became aware of the etheric records, the truth of the mystic would be discovered.

So it was left to the mystic/scribes to create written documents to hold the masses in a fear-driven state. The written words offered just enough hope and respect to lead the commoner to believe that he could attain only a limited level of holiness. This kept him in a position of subservience. The words were presented in such a way that, if heeded only as prescribed, a path to the Creator could be opened to him.

Let it be known that the writings of that time also contained the locations of many things. Amongst them were worldly riches, and information of the Creator's star constellations by which travel on sea and land could be successfully accomplished. There were also writings that spoke of civilizations that were more highly advanced than the human civilization.

In essence, all the information that was needed to evolve to new levels of awareness had the possibility of being reduced to the written word. So why were the few who were aware of these writings so unwilling to share them with the masses?

Since it was designed that only the mystic/scribes knew how to read and write, they carried with them an air of mystery and power. They exercised their power over the people by deciding to whom and to what extent the information was doled out. The mystic/scribes controlled all knowledge. Thus, you can see how the written word could be misconstrued to create any desired outcome.

Church and State

The emperors sensed that they were losing control, and fear gripped even the most dull-minded of them. A growing concern was that the mystics/scribes might turn on them. Meanwhile, the mystics/scribes, took every opportunity to assure the emperors as leaders. Their plan was for the emperors to be held responsible to the masses for all that they, the mystics, devised.

What came next? Religion.

Religion in its most popular form teaches from fear. The mystics, who knew the power of the written word, used it to their advantage. In their writings, they portrayed God as a fear-inspiring, all-powerful energy. Their next step was to designate only one figurehead, themselves, through which God would communicate with humans. With only one recognized connection to God, it is easy to see how control was taken to the next level.

Having established themselves as the official connection to God, the mystics/scribes who now became the new religious leaders went about establishing their own form of empire. A perceived separation was created between matters of religion and the affairs of state, and the commoners were glad to be free of the emperor. Little did the commoners realize that the true rulers, the mystics/spiritual advisors/ explorers/scribes—now turned religious leaders—were still in complete charge of the empire. Why? Simply because the mystics continued to hold all recorded knowledge within their control.

The mystic/religious leaders began building churches and creating new laws. No pilgrimage would be endeavored without the sanction of the church. No lands were accepted into the realm without the blessing of the church. No laws of the emperors were enforced without the authorization of the church. Everything had to pass the scrutiny of the religious leaders who were still the official spiritual advisors to the emperors.

If the mystic/religious leaders needed to create a war to keep their power secure, they would pit one emperor against another. Indeed, who wouldn't support a military campaign? On the surface, all appeared to win. If the emperor or king were successful, he would glean great profits. If the commoner worked hard at building armaments, he earned more money. The unfortunate exception was the soldier in battle who usually lost his life—in the name of God and emperor.

Let us not forget that the wars did much to curb excessive population. Let us consider the fact that only the fittest males were sent to do battle. This might explain why the weaker male rulers who remained at home exerted excessive authoritarian powers to maintain control.

The emperors never suspected that their religious leaders worked together behind the scenes. It was still a closely guarded secret that the mystics/religious leaders were in collaboration. But, by maintaining the appearance of separation, they were guaranteed a win, regardless of which emperor was victorious in battle.

Empires were thriving. The mystics, now religious leaders, continued to travel or send their representatives to far-off lands in search of great riches. Exploiting both people and lands with the backing of their emperor and their God, the religious leaders held onto the best for their own empire, the church.

What if, my friends, that cycle continues to this day?

The Religionist Feels Threatened

In the far-reaching parts of the world, the mystic/religious leaders encountered their counterparts who had no ties to emperors' courts. These counterparts can be described as "the pure mystics."

Never having had to play the games of control and fear, the pure mystics were free to raise their metaphysical powers to new levels of awareness. They had the freedom to experience greater and greater awakenings. These pure mystics learned to evolve in harmony with all that surrounded them. Being pure, they had no hidden agenda. They were open to share their knowledge with their mystic counterparts who had long before diminished their own metaphysical powers.

The pure mystics were sharing their knowledge with the people and had gained a following amongst the commoners. The people reported having witnessed miracles performed by these mystics, who also were regarded as healers.

Suddenly, the pure mystic/healers were a threat to the mystic/religious leaders. But the pure mystics took no interest because their powers were a result of their love. They knew that their powers were greater than those of their counterparts, but had no desire to prove themselves better.

Realizing the power of these pure mystic/healers, the rulers of both the state and the church needed to act quickly. For if the pure mystic/healers were allowed to perform miracles and the lowest of commoners discovered that they could commune with all creation, all power structures would breakdown. So, it was decided that the pure mystic/healers would be invited to join forces with the religious leaders. The response from the pure mystics was clear: They would not join in any efforts to control the people. Instead, the pure mystics began to speak out amongst the people and admonished them for being controlled.

Again, the response by the church leaders was swift. Any pure mystic/healer not subscribing to the power and control of the religious leaders was immediately branded as an enemy of the church. Such mystic/healers were judged as evil and were hunted down and slaughtered.

The Grandest of Examples

Books have been written, and will continue to be written, that shed light on how the history of humankind has been put into written form. Clearly, just because one is able to hold up a book and show the world the written word does not mean its writings are accurate and complete. In fact, as this work is being completed, changes to history are being registered in many places.

Let's look at how one book came to be written.

In the 1500's, a gathering of men was formed to sift through countless scrolls that had been written to describe the world of religion. Given the task of compiling the materials into one complete religious work, they encountered texts written on almost every conceivable possibility. Some texts were found badly torn and battered. Some writings were barely discernible. More often than not, gaps were filled in by the writer when the materials were undecipherable. Yet from this gathering, the most highly recognized format on which many religions base their beliefs today was offered to the world—and because it was offered as the written word, few would question it. The Bible was now set to guide the world.

How did this take place? Beyond the technical problems of undecipherable or damaged material, much of the available text was dropped. In many cases, destroyed. For instance, if a document surfaced that countered the thinking of the time, with a simple spark of a flame, it was removed. When the material considered out of alignment was taken to the religious leaders for explanation, they would lead the questioner to think that the material was insignificant. The documents were then placed in a special archive, established to house these so-called meaningless materials. We are now aware that all has not been brought to light. In fact, little has been revealed.

What Is the Next Level?

Hopefully as you are reading what has been presented here, a sense of something familiar has awakened within you. It may seem as if you had read this work before. This is because each evolving soul committed to Mother Earth has the chance to remember—to recall that a system of fear, methodically placed in alignment with the unseen forces of so-called darkness, truly has no power. All are to be reminded that light, of which humanity is made, is the total experience used to complete the journey.

In order to recognize where you will ultimately arrive, you, like the pure mystic, must have a true understanding of the matrix world that surrounds you. The Creator, in Its infinite power to heal, has allowed for the human evolutionary being the most precious gift, the gift of thought. Each human is in the beginning stages of a total transformation through thought.

What if, my friends, it is the birthright of all to heal from the illusionary separation. You will discover that each human's meticulously designed outward appearance is really a thought form of highly vibrating light particles amassed into a functionary lesson plan. You will find that each plan includes no restrictions, only the truth of the Divine Creator. The hoax of doom and gloom that the world has become so engrossed in will be revealed in the light of Truth, Trust, and Passion.

The only question might be, Why now? The answer, my friends, is simply, You are ready.

* * *

Questions and Answers:

Q: What is the role of religion in human history?

Kirael: My friends, religious belief systems have been used to sever the oneness of humankind. Otherwise, why would we need all the "isms," such as Catholicism, Shintoism, Hinduism, to define one Creator, if not to have something to disagree about? The reality of this statement is brought to fullness when you look up the word "religion" in Webster's Dictionary. From Latin, you will find "religio," which means religious practice or supernatural constraint. If you pursue it further, you will find that the likely root word is "religare," which means to restrain or tie back.

What a perfect scenario: one God, many ways of defining this energy, and power in the hands of those who controlled what was written about this energy.

Q: How did the Dark Ages in human history occur?

Kirael: Clarity must be brought to the era spanning the years 200 BC to 200 AD. It was a time when the human race reverted to a point where people no longer believed in themselves. Some may regard this period as the darkest times in recorded history.

Some six hundred years before Jesus began his mission, another trinity had formed. The trinity consisted of the teachings of Buddha (spirituality), Pythagoras (morality), and Isaiah (physicality). Their collective teachings shared that the human world had a direct connection to the Creator's Light.

In that same time period, many great library systems were established. We speak here of the most notable libraries of the time, the Alexandrian libraries. The libraries were renowned for having within their collection between 700,000 to 800,000 scrolls or records. Within those records, the reader could become enlightened to the possibilities and realities of a world beyond their own simple existence.

The Alexandrian libraries included documents from great thinkers that facilitated the evolution of humankind. There was information on scrolls which disproved the theory that the world was flat. Knowledge of the Earth's movement around the sun and the expanding solar system could be also found. There were also journals of great voyages to places known today as the continents of Africa and South America. Remember, this was in 200 BC, long before the time Jesus walked the Earth.

Some fifty years before Christ's teachings, those in power began the systematic burning of these libraries in the professed name of protecting humankind from itself. They feared that such a vast collection of recorded knowledge would destroy their power structures. Hence, orders were given to destroy the entire library system.

Each phase of the systematic burning of the scrolls was connected to an event where humanity began to gain more awareness and assume their God-like essence. The burning of the Alexandrian libraries would be final around the sixth century. To the best of present-day knowledge, only as few as 40,000 of these scrolls were saved from destruction, copied or secretly stored for future use. A number of them are stored deep in the Vatican archives to this day.

By the time Jesus walked the Earth, society was plummeting into a world of secrecy. What was learned was harbored and shared secretly with others of like mind. What one knew, one didn't reveal. People feared that those who destroyed the libraries would also seek out those who were aware of the contents of the destroyed records. It was indeed a time of darkness for the world.

Here one begins to recognize how the rhetoric of a mystical messenger, such as Jesus, could unnerve those trying to hold onto their power. If Jesus' teachings were accurate, those in power who perpetuated the teachings of a vindictive and judgmental God, omnipresent but beyond direct contact, were afraid to have that truth revealed. Without this misrepresentation of God, the rulers had little control over the minds of the people.

Q: Did women study in the Alexandrian libraries?

Kirael: Throughout history, the females have allowed themselves to appear as simple mortals, accepting their world as subservient to that of the males. It would best be brought to light that this is a falsehood.

While the men were busying themselves conquering the world, education was offered to only a few. So, it was decided that the women would be sent to study in the Alexandrian libraries and pass this information on to the males.

In no time, these women became intoxicated, if you will, with what they were discovering. They found in the multitude of scrolls realities they had never imagined existed before. To their astonishment, they realized they were being exposed to the knowingness found within the All That Is.

The women's job was to share the contents of the Alexandrian scrolls with the male leaders of the time. As they did so, the men became afraid. The male world realized the potential of the knowledge the women had acquired, and wanted to claim it as their own. They quickly saw how the women had become far more learned than their best mystics and soothsayers. And worse, the newly gained knowledge was contrary to the world as they had come to believe it. This created panic among them.

When the truth is fully known, it will show that it was the women who appropriated as many scrolls as they could for safekeeping. The women cherished the magnitude of their learning and initiated the process of secretly sending scrolls into other parts of the world.

This period of time is likely the most influential in the evolution of the learned female. The meticulous manner in which they garnered the information from the Alexandrian libraries was used to ensure the world of a feminine, emotion-based, influence throughout all history.

As difficult as it may be for the males to hear this: it is truth that without the influence of the females in that time period, the world would likely have been brought to extinction many times over.

Q: Are you willing to define the term "secret government"?

Kirael: Assuming this will not be found on the cutting room floor, it would be my pleasure.

First of all, it makes sense to look at the words themselves: "secret," meaning that which is held from the populace; and "government," meaning that which is something else being held from the populace.

It would be easy to place a mythological monster on a shiny pedestal and call it the "secret government" for all to scorn. Yet, if the chapter you have just read has any validity at all, you will understand that most of what the human world fears is placed there by those who need to control.

It is easier for humans to blame their problems on something that has no tangible presence than it is to accept the fact that they have relinquished control.

Why is masterminding not taught in schools? Why is it labeled as mind-tampering in some cases? Who has the most to lose if "you, the people" begin to understand that masterminding can create any reality, or illusion, that is conceivable to a mind that knows no limits? Who then has control?

For so long, the name "secret government" has conjured up fear in the minds of many. As long as it appears that some unseen force is in control and that the world cannot be changed, it makes sense to carry on as in the past. Today, however, too many questions are being asked. You, the people, are creating new truths, such as, everyone has the Creator-given birthright to heal their fear-imposed limitations. Thus, it is no longer the collective understanding that the human race is under the control of unseen forces.

The angels, guides, and your galactic brothers and sisters are willing to show you the path beyond the third-dimensional thought matrix. They are not willing to walk it for you, but will continue to light the path of understanding. In this way, each will determine his or her chosen arrival in the new light of the Shift.

4

Thought: A Few Thinking for the Masses

Kirael's Numerology:
On a "4" day, be very conscious of your thinking processes. Keep your thoughts extremely positive, because in the world of thought, they can readily be manifested in any direction.

Author's Insights:

For centuries, the same lesson plans have repeated themselves time after time, but on an ever-expanding scale. Some of us in years past, myself included, have been bold enough to lay the fault for our regrettable creations on the Creator, or we focus our problems on others. In essence, we always seem to have someone or something to point the finger of blame at when things do not go as we planned.

When all else fails, some of us blame society or "the secret government" because that allows us the luxury to pretend that what is happening is beyond our control. If we gave credence to this "secret society," then it could be described as "the power that the human world has created so that humanity may have a reason to not move forward in love."

Approximately 2000 years ago, society became weary of fighting wars that could not be seen, and of listening to rhetoric that could not be understood. It was a time when one man, Jesus, was made a symbol to the world. His life demonstrated what could happen if one person created too big of a ripple in the water, and how one man's teachings could be compromised by others to rule the masses. What follows is an explanation of how the initial mission of the church was transformed into an institution. A place where initially all could learn of the Creator's Light in freedom, the church later proclaimed its superiority and justified the killings of human light in the name of God.

Kirael Speaks:

Two thousand years ago, wars were raging, and the two most powerful countries were barely able to finance the ongoing conflicts. On one side were the Romans, who by nature were a conquering nation that wanted the entire world to submit to their control. Believing that dominance was the only way to subject others to their influence, they spent most of their wealth on the accumulation of military power. The technology that they had so proudly introduced to the world was utilized to conquer all who were in their path.

On the other side were the Greeks. They were the most opportunistic people that the Romans encountered as enemies. The Grecian society was rich in technology, with an abundance of assets which enabled them to wage continuous battles on numerous fronts. Their culture spawned great thinkers who engaged in complex military campaigns and gathered great knowledge from those they conquered.

The rulers of both nations knew that vast wealth could continue to be amassed as long as wars were being fought and the people were kept in fear.

The leaders created the illusion that the enemy would destroy the commoners' villages, unless the armies were kept strong and ready for action. By harvesting the food and melding the armaments for military purposes, the commoner was made to believe that he played an important role in protecting his world. Unfortunately, he was left with the most meager of resources to survive on, while the wealthy gained more riches as the wars raged on.

Even in those times, the need for funds to sustain the war machine was unquenchable. Taxes were raised at such a rate that the commoner did not have time to understand the calculations of one levy before a new one was implemented. The punishment for not paying taxes was swift and harsh enough to leave lasting impressions on those who contemplated such an act.

On the surface, it appeared that all the money raised was used to outfit the armies, so few, if any, questions were asked. What was truly taking place, was the establishment of a hierarchy of world dominance.

It was being arranged on levels so subtle that even the so-called rulers were unaware of what was really happening.

At the same time, the people were kept busy guarding against what they perceived to be threats of world dominance. For the most part, they fought against forces that they could not see or were unaware existed. They were not allowed time to question how their money was spent. This was the establishment of a system that would rule the world until this day.

Not To Worry - He is Only a Man

On another front, something new was growing in strength. Small groups of individuals were talking of a young man who was creating a stir. He was speaking of human powers believed then to be held only by God.

Who was this daring young man of humble origins, preaching on the shores and in the smallest of towns? It appeared that this self-appointed prophet had gathered a small band of followers and was preaching about impossible dreams. The followers were just ordinary citizens who were mainly fishermen and common laborers, as well as the poor and downtrodden.

To those in power, this preacher and his supporters could be viewed as nothing more than a small thorn in their side. Despite powerful rumors, the rulers thought that a man who showed no interest in gaining wealth could not cause much trouble. Concerns about this "holy man" were laid to rest when it was learned that he surrounded himself with females and sought their counsel. The rulers asked, How much influence could one man preaching of love and healing have if only the commoners and females showed interest? Rather than take him seriously, he became a laughing matter.

In fact, neither Romans nor Greeks had time to focus on anything that did not contribute to filling their coffers, because their wars were becoming increasingly uncontrollable.

Then the scenario began to change. This preacher, called Jesus, gathered more and more followers. The followers were no longer the poor and downtrodden. Those of wealth were listening to the talk of miracles that Jesus was performing. To the dismay of the rulers, money normally reserved for war machines was now being spent to send family members with serious or terminal illnesses to Jesus, with the hopes of being healed. People from all walks of life were traveling great distances to be in the presence of his light.

The poor and wealthy, in large masses, were listening to Jesus talk about a Great Shift, and of vast changes that were to take place. He spoke of self-empowerment. With conviction, he assured those who would listen that all people were equal in the Light of the Creator. This was a new concept, especially to the wealthy who could lose all they owned by the swift stroke of a knife-wielding centurion or by the quill of a taxman.

With the wealthy showing interest in the teachings of Jesus, the rulers discovered that the money that would normally belong in the coffers of their war treasury was redirected to further the work of Jesus. This could not be allowed.

The Threat of Change

When the rulers went to the seers or chief priests to seek counsel on the man called Jesus, the priests would not speak in truth. To acknowledge Jesus' power was to overshadow their own. They knew that they could not compete with Jesus, so they simply proceeded to deny the existence of his powers. If a ruler approached a priest to inquire about the man called Jesus, the priest would convince him that the powers of Jesus were false.

By the time the leaders awoke to the virtue of the powers of Jesus, he had already gained the following of multitudes. When Jesus was accused before the Roman leaders, they realized their authority was being seriously challenged. It was clear to both priests and rulers that they were about to lose their authority. They knew that they would have to act quickly, even harshly, to maintain their dominance.

Jesus was brought before Pilate, the governor of Judea. Pilate questioned Jesus, found him not guilty of wrongdoing, then released him. The chief priest, firmly determined to destroy Jesus, admonished Pilate not to release him. The chief priest insisted that he order Jesus be put to death. Finding no justifiable reason to do so, Pilate searched for ways to avoid the judgment.

Learning that Jesus was originally from Galilee, Pilate sent Jesus swiftly to the jurisdiction ruled by Herod. That way, Pilate avoided putting to death a man he knew to be innocent of any punishable crime. Pilate felt relieved, for it would not be his duty to take the life of this kindly gentleman. In truth, Pilate was so enthralled by this man's energy that he quietly prayed for a way to spare Jesus' life, even if it meant suffering the wrath of his seers.

Thus, Pilate was shocked when Herod returned Jesus to him. Upon listening to the charges against Jesus, Herod, also, saw no cause to put Jesus to death. After counsel with the high priest, Herod sent Jesus back to Pilate on the premise that Jesus must be dealt with by the one who was responsible for his capture.

Pilate held counsel with his wife. She told Pilate that a visitor in her dream warned her of a disaster. Pilate must release this one called Jesus or much harm would befall his kingdom.

What was Pilate to do? Following the counsel of his high priest advisors, a foolproof plan was devised. It was agreed that the people would decide the life or death of this mystical man. Pilate scoured the dungeons to find the worst of the imprisoned criminals. He then had this criminal stand alongside Jesus in front of the crowds and allowed the people to choose who should live and who should die. By doing it this way, Pilate's hands remained clean of blame. The will of the people would determine the outcome. However, the high priests left nothing to chance. Little did Pilate know the crowd that gathered was handpicked and paid by Pilate's high priest advisors to condemn Jesus to death.

Imagine Pilate's shock when he learned that the crowd chose to have Jesus put to death, and the imprisoned murderer set free. Pilate remained convinced that he was not responsible for this judgement because the people had spoken. On that very day, humankind was denied the beauty of experiencing a great shift in awareness.

Jesus' Death: The End or The Beginning?

Jesus' teachings of love and healing empowered the people. Through the example of his life, the people believed that they could commune directly with God. All were seen as equal in the Creator's Light. He reminded all that awakening to the fullness of love through the energy of healing was the answer to the world's ills.

Jesus' teachings caused people to question all the things they had accepted as law. The people wanted the freedom to heal in love, while those in power wanted to maintain control.

The Discipleship of Peter

After the death of Jesus, many people continued to follow his teachings, but few had the impact on the world as did Peter and Paul. Although both appeared to be presenting the same message of Christianity, their writings to the Christian Church demonstrated different agendas and led to two distinctly different outcomes.

Almost immediately after Peter was anointed by Jesus to lead through love and healing, his life would be dedicated to sharing the messages that Jesus had brought forth. He began the formation of churches for all to understand that each was in the God's Light. He intended the church to be a place where all appreciated the love of the Creator at their own pace and understood that all was perfect in its own creation. Like that of Jesus' teachings, Peter's ministry was based on remembering to be in love and that the capacity to heal was within all people.

The Leadership of Paul

What follows on the life of Paul is brought to light so that you, the reader, may unveil your own knowingness and discover your own truth.

History shows that Paul (known as Saul in his early years) came from a wealthy family. His schooling was of the highest possible standards of that time. At an early age, he was schooled in the teachings of one called Gamaliel. Under Gamaliel's teachings, which came solely from the scriptures of the Old Testament, the students were shown how to use the written words to their best advantage. They learned to formulate any outcome they desired. Because the word was written, this made it non-negotiable. Remember, few of that time had the privilege of mastering the skills of reading and writing.

Initially, Paul used the knowledge gained from his schooling to speak out against Jesus. Paul claimed that the teachings of Jesus went against the teachings of the scriptures of the Old Testament. He maintained for many years that Jesus was speaking untruths. Paul rejected Jesus' teachings because he knew they would cause people to challenge the existing power structure. Jesus' idea of oneness with the Creator did not require a firm control over the people's actions. If the people had a direct communication with the Source, then what would become of the prevailing hierarchy?

In his early years, Paul opposed Jesus' teachings so fiercely that he was feared by many. In collaboration with the rulers, he persecuted and put to death anyone who believed in Jesus' teachings.

One day, Paul's life changed as a result of what can only be interpreted as divine intervention. He recounts in the Bible, the story of his journey to Damascus where many of Jesus' followers had gathered. Having heard that there was a large population of Christians in Damascus preaching in Jewish temples, he had immediately set out for the city. It was his intention to punish those who would openly demonstrate against the authorities.

On his way there, Paul encountered a woman who spoke in tongues (likely using channeled information). She told him of events that were to unfold in the future. In disbelief, Paul dismissed her as an evil person who had a personal agenda, then continued on his journey.

Soon after the woman departed, Paul began to experience a power he had never known. So overwhelming was this new sensation that his ability to use his five senses was diminished. In moments, Paul's entire life flashed before him. He saw in the course of his life that he had not followed his heart. In that instant, he was given an opportunity to see the outcome of his life if he continued on this path. Thus, he made new choices that would change the world.

Paul's Agenda

The leaders of the time hoped to thwart a growing separation between the people and those in authority. It had become clear that the new movement of Christianity, following the death of Jesus, had far-reaching influence upon the masses. The people were seeking a new leader to fill the spiritual void that Jesus' death had created.

Paul realized that he could placate the rulers and the masses simultaneously by merging the teachings of Gamaliel and the teachings of Jesus. From that moment on, Paul began to use Jesus' life and teachings as his power base to accomplish this.

Paul began to anoint those who came before him in the name of Jesus, the Christ, as John the Baptist had done before him. There was a significant difference, however, in how his practice of this ritual was viewed. In the eyes of the rulers and the wealthy, John the Baptist was a common man with no social upbringing. The rulers saw him as being disruptive, and he was labeled as a troublemaker. Paul, on the other hand, was an influential aristocrat, learned, and articulate. His status in society allowed him to use the words of Jesus to appease the Christian followers, yet assure the wealthy of their position in power.

Paul realized how Jesus' words became more poignant as he allowed the enlightenment of the Christ Consciousness to embody his essence. He witnessed how the power of Jesus' words and deeds inspired the people. Thus, with his extensive education, Paul saw the opportunity to adapt Jesus' teachings for what he saw as the good of all.

Paul believed that his writings on the life and teachings of Jesus would reduce the bloodshed and bridge the gap between the followers of Christianity and the rulers. Through his gift of eloquence, Paul formulated the written words to fit the outcome he desired. He negotiated an acceptable path between the conflicting groups by leading the masses to believe that a separation of Church and State existed. Yet, a veiled hierarchy of power between the Church and State was maintained to guide the masses. It was Paul's words that shaped the teachings of the New Testament and led to the marriage of Church and State.

Those who look hard and deep enough will see how Paul's choices to revise the teachings of Jesus shaped the world of religion as seen today. You might ask yourself these questions to awaken to your inner knowing of spirit. How is it possible to believe that anyone would claim to be superior to others in the name of Jesus? How could a sword be raised in the name of Jesus to murder a brother or sister to prove that one religion was better than another? If you truly understood the light of Jesus' teachings, would you not offer the other compassion without any intention of harm? From the heart, would not each know this power? After all, Jesus preached that all were of the same Light of the Creator.

Remember that Jesus said, "Whatsoever I do, so shall you." In his Truth, you will realize that it is the Trust of the Creator's Light that gave birth to the Passion of human essence. And when Jesus shared, as stated in the Bible at Matthew 18:20, "For where two or three are gathered together in my name, there am I in the midst of them," you will understand that in the trinity of Truth, Trust, and Passion, the collective consciousness of the people will reestablish the light on Mother Earth. Together, in the "thought" mastermind of love and healing the human world will ascend.

✶ ✶ ✶

Questions and Answers:

Q: How did the Church maintain power over the people?

Kirael: Keeping the people uneducated and ignorant was beneficial in maintaining the church hierarchy. The church leaders taught what was in their best interest to further their goals. They decided what the masses were to be told. The way they disseminated the information to the people maintained a certainty that no one questioned.

People were kept in ignorance and used to fill the ranks of the armies. Only the wealthy had the time and fortune to attain any formal education. This ensured that the people heard only what the leaders wanted them to hear.

The church's practice of confession was a way for the clergy to be kept informed on the workings and understanding of the masses. The information they gained in confidentiality in the confessional was used to persecute those who listened to the teachings of the more progressive spiritualists.

It was believed that only the highest levels of clergy were able to talk to God. The ultimate power was delegated to the Pope. This established a seemingly all-powerful leader whose sole responsibility was to inform the people of the evolution of the world. What many failed to recognize is that even in the world today, the Pope, along with the presidents of most countries, are literally powerless.

Q: If the time of duality, or yin and yang, is now shifting to amplify the thought of trinities, how can we see the work of Peter and Paul trinitized?

Kirael: I have spoken many times of the apparent differences in the journeys of these two, yet there is one common thread. They were both aware of a great awakening taking place here on Earth.

They differed, however, in how they chose to amplify their knowing. Peter chose to create a house of God to enlighten the path for those wishing to return to the Creator essence. He viewed each person as an equal in the eyes of God. Paul, on the other hand, felt the need to control the masses through an established hierarchy of power. Their work may be trinitized by the love they shared for the all-powerful energy of their Creator.

Q: Peter and Paul were masters at practicing the art of masterminding. How does this it work?

Kirael: It is best to see a mastermind as a collective energy of two or more people who hold truth in light. Each mastermind group has the potential of achieving great success on varying levels. This is determined by the measure of passion each person holds to the mastermind thought.

Every thought that is brought to light by a human has the birthright to manifest into reality. One of the checks and balances of the human vibration is the need for emotions. When you consider that one completes thousands of thoughts on your dimension in a minute, there must be a stopgap to achieve any kind of focus. If not, the world would be in a constant state of confusion. This is where emotions come in.

When a thought is perceived and enhanced by the element of passion, it begins the journey of evolution. The length of time it takes to magnetize the thought energy into manifestation depends on the degree of emotion that the thought was sent out with. Once the thought finds similar particle energy, it draws as much of this energy as possible to its own light. Then the thought is manifested in this conscious reality.

Let us use the example of a thought that has sufficient passion to become a reality. Then add to it the other people holding the same thought. The collective passion that is created energizes the thought or mastermind, achieving that reality in a short time.

An important key in masterminding is to remember that a chain is only as strong as its weakest link. When one person in a mastermind group does not truly believe in the outcome that is being masterminded, one of two things results. The potential outcome is weakened. Second, the mastermind group continues, but the one with doubts must be willing to leave the group in love and return only when he or she can be in complete alignment with the rest of the group.

When the human world loses its fear of the mastermind process and understands its true powers, life will enter a new level of awareness.

Q: Is the so-called secret government a mastermind?

Kirael: The secret government might be best described as a conglomerate of beliefs conceived in less-than-loving thoughts. Through its passion to control, it gives people a reason to relinquish their own self-control.

The secret government has existed since humanity allowed fear to rule its conscious thought process. The reason I prefer not to discuss this unseen force is because talking about it amplifies its energy. It gains greater strength from the weakness of opposing bodies of thought. In other words, while the masses attempt to discover who is in control of this energy, that same energy is adding strength to its already diminished light force.

Q: Could you speak of the mastermind of Hitler?

Kirael: Hitler's mastermind was created from a small core of humans. His original intent was passion; the passion to create a perfect reality. However, the mastermind was absent of love, and therefore, the passion turned into fear. This is the most conclusive example of a fear-based mastermind that was only stopped when a stronger mastermind overtook it.

In his reality of "non-love," Hitler relied on the mastermind of the people and the forces of darkness that surrounded him to sustain his horrific reality. Now when I say darkness, I am literally referring to the light particles that were strained of their light. Because Hitler had closed himself off from the Creator's Light, the darkened energy of fear was fed back into the mastermind. This self-perpetuation of the doom and gloom continued to amplify the mastermind. In this process, the most horrendous acts of the world were committed.

Should they be excused? Never. Should they be learned from? Always. The lesson to be learned, my friend, is that it is possible to create a darkened force within a light vibrational entity such as Mother Earth and her inhabitants, but it takes people unwilling to honor love to create it.

It will take the lightworkers of the world to create masterminds of love and healing to bring forth the changes in Truth, Trust, and Passion.

Q: You have said, "A mastermind is only as strong as its weakest link." How can people in a mastermind support the person who is recognized as the weakest link?

Kirael: Well, I will spell it, L-O-V-E. Love is what caused this person to be the weakest link, but it is misguided love. When a person is guided from the vibration of "less than," he or she creates limitations mastermind because it becomes self-serving.

So here is what I suggest you do. If you have a mastermind of love and you feel a weakness, let love prevail. First, experience the energy that resonates least to the mastermind as your mirror reflection. Hence, when you look at the so-called weakest link, you recognize your own weakness. This will show you the reasons manifestation is so slow. If you are able to acknowledge and heal the fears of any self-imposed limitations, then extraordinary things will begin to happen.

The members of the mastermind must commit themselves to aiding the weakest link that all of you are a part of. Love that person in fullness. Most often, you will find this difficult to do, for this person will attempt to draw your energies to its security level of self-limitation. If this energy grows, then your mastermind falters.

Before you let that happen, my friends, provide the weakest link every bit of healing, and I suggest a complete four-body healing. If that person is unwilling to heal into love, he or she will maintain its level no matter how low it is. Continue to express your kindness and compassion, and be in love enough to release that person from the mastermind. Then, offer the energy of the weakest link into the Creator's Light. Likely, you will see this link disappear and the chain of the mastermind will reform itself stronger than ever.

5

Love: Jesus and the Female Disciples

Kirael's Numerology:
On a "5" day, watch for anything around you that can resonate in
love and take advantage of if. Be in love on a "5" day and feel love
surrounding you. When you choose love as the foundation of each
decision, all comes to perfection in light.

Author's Insights:

It becomes evident as the truths begin to unfold that in one human lifetime, Jesus lived two very defined lesson plans. The first of Jesus' lesson plans, which took place in his youth, was to fully experience the human journey. It was about mastering the common human conditions of worldly goods, lack of money, and the highs and lows of human emotions.

One might expect that Jesus' experiences were more dramatic than the average human experience, and in part, that is true. We can say the same for challenges that he had to face. Still, Jesus' lesson plans unfolded basically in the same manner as any human. As he gained awareness from each experience learned, he came to the conclusion that all people are in constant control of every aspect of their journey, regardless of how it appears.

For the second lesson plan of Jesus' life, he would live in his adult years as the "Son Light" of the Creator. During the years of his incarnation, Jesus would gain the powers to move within the forces of light. He would live in completeness the life plan that the Creator had allowed him to fulfill in his journey of love and healing.

Jesus found it natural to work with the females in his life. So why does written history not show the powerful impressions the females left in his life? We will find that if the truths of Jesus' writings were discovered, the writings of the men who were responsible to synopsize his life would be revised. This would literally change history for all time.

Kirael Speaks:

The female experience with Jesus can be explained by contrasting the women's lives with those of the male population. Then, as it is often the case now, the males were fully absorbed in the divide-and-conquer mode with little patience for realizing the full journey. Let us just say that males tended to predominantly utilize the physical and mental parts of their energies, while females tended to focus on balancing all four bodies (physical, emotional, mental, and spiritual). In that light, females sought every possibility of healing on deepest levels. The women quickly aligned to the true message of Jesus: If each would focus on discovering love at its highest vibration, all would be enlightened through healing.

The Female Disciples

When Jesus walked the Earth some two thousand years ago, females would have been ranked third by value of necessity. First were the male children who were valued as most vital because they assured a perpetuation of the family line. A close second was the mule, for it was viewed as a symbol of wealth. Then, the female would find her place at a distant third.

This does not sound very complimentary. Yet, it does serve to show why women have been relegated to attaining their own accomplishments behind the scenes. Dismaying as this may seem, women maintain a behind-the-scenes presence in some of the most influential dealings concerning the path of human development, even in today's society. Their contributions are sadly under-recognized.

The women surrounding Jesus were his teachers, supporters and confidants. In fact, if Leonardo da Vinci, who painted "The Last Supper," had turned around and painted the scene behind him, we would have seen the table where Jesus' twelve female disciples were seated.

Jesus' Grandmother

Before we begin speaking of Jesus' mother, Mary, we may be reminded that even she had a mother. There is little mention of her in recorded history. However, one of the many books that never "made it" in the selection process of King James' version of the Bible was the scroll that spoke of Mary's mother. This scroll described her as being barren of child until she conceived Mary in her early eighties.

She was well schooled in the Essene tradition for the better part of her adult life. The spiritual group known as the Essenes may possibly have been the forerunners of the metaphysically-oriented humans of today. While the pharaohs and emperors of that time concentrated on hoarding vast riches, the Essenes attempted to establish a firm union between the physical and spiritual worlds.

Despite the efforts of the rulers at the time of Jesus to cast doubt on those who were not in alignment with their schemes, the Essenes were privately sought out often to perform healings on the poorest as well as the wealthiest, especially when all else failed. They were healers who focused on non-traditional ways in caring for the less fortunate and the ill. They shared their skills with all that would listen. The grandmother of Jesus was said to have been highly recognized as a devoted and caring healer. Much of the healing techniques that Jesus would use are directly related to the teachings of the Essene traditions.

How exciting it is to offer a fascinating bit of information here about someone hardly spoken of in "authorized" history books, and to see how history takes on an entirely new and vibrant reality! Until now, many have even accepted Mary, the mother of Jesus, as a simple daughter of a commoner. However, you can see now how highly influential these mothers were in Jesus' life.

Mother Mary

As I bring forth information on this most beautiful energy, there are those who might view Mary's watchfulness over Jesus as almost obsessive in the early stages of his life.

Imagine if you can, being visited by Spirit in the middle of the night and being told that a most auspicious event is about to unfold.

Imagine being told that the child you are going to birth into reality is coming to save all humanity. Nothing could prepare you for such drama. How then does one watch over this special being of light? One can only wonder.

It did come to pass that one day, as the young Jesus was playing like any other lad his age, he lost his balance and hurt himself. Can you imagine the horror Mary must have experienced when she saw Jesus lying there with blood running from his cut?

Frozen in fear, Mary cried out to the other children to run and bid Joseph, her husband, to come home. The moment Joseph was told of Jesus' accident, he began to pray to the angels, imploring them to be with his son. As he hastened to reach Jesus' side, Joseph heard a beautiful voice saying that his prayers had been answered and all was well. The voice also suggested that his concerns might be better placed with Mary, for her own energy was in total dishevelment.

Upon his arrival, Joseph found Jesus already wanting to return to play with his young mates, just as the angels had said. Mary was still fraught with horror. Overcome with love for Mary, Joseph sat with her while she returned to a pleasant space. As Joseph waited, he became aware of what sounded like a conversation taking place in a far-off realm. Instantly, he knew that the angels were consoling Mary.

He heard Mary ask the angels why she felt so helpless at a time when her son needed her the most. The answer came swiftly.

"Dear one," a voice said, "now you can see that this Light of the Creator is to walk in the world of humans. He must be allowed to see, feel, and be aware of the most beautiful experiences here on the human level. How could he know the pain of the people if not to feel it first-hand? How was he to know about healing if not allowed to experience the process from within?"

The angels went on to share with Mary that Jesus' journey was to be filled with human experiences on all four levels of awareness: physical, emotional, mental, and spiritual. She was to allow that unfolding to take place. Only then would a lasting impression of the human experience be deeply imbedded in Jesus' mind. Finally, Mary was reminded that one of the most important teachings her son would impart to the world was that every aspect of the journey needs to be experienced for the completion of the life lesson.

Even with the counsel of these angels, who were her constant companions, Mary would labor painfully each time the slightest drama would unfold in Jesus' life. Many times she wondered what would happen if she could do nothing to help her son. You can only imagine how this thought would shatter her heart the day of Jesus' crucifixion, while she stood at her son's feet watching his life force ebb away.

Martha

Some of Jesus' fondest memories of his childhood years were the times he was left in the care of the one he knew of as Aunt Martha. In her home, Jesus found the one place where he was free from the watchful eye of his mother.

Fully honoring the importance of Jesus to the world, Martha attempted to influence his early life by presenting him with beauty in every aspect of his surroundings. She was determined to see that Jesus experienced all the beauty that the Creator had gifted to the human world.

Martha's steadfast reminders to Jesus of love and healing most certainly influenced this young master's outlook on life. Each time Jesus allowed his thinly veiled ego to gain presence, she reminded him that one day his every action, spoken or simply observed, would be left to interpretation by the masses.

Just as importantly, Martha spent many hours asking Jesus profound questions of this world and beyond. Jesus' responses created a wonderment of possibilities. Already at this young age, his dialogue was in parables. It seemed that his answers had more than one meaning. And Martha was always left to stretch her world of knowing to limits never before experienced.

It would not be long before Martha began to recognize the impact that Jesus' teachings would have on humanity. It was by hearing Jesus' words such as "healing" and the "All That Is," that she knew of the existence of what he was speaking.

Jesus would speak of the female population as being on an equal basis with the male population. Martha was an advanced thinker of that time, so she knew Jesus' views would not set well with those who expected the female to play an extremely subservient role to the male. It was a time when the male protected his role through powerful displays of manhood and overlooked the importance of the female.

Often Martha sensed Jesus understood issues on levels that were not resonating with those in power. This would cause her to be concerned for his safety. She reminded Jesus that the world might likely find his teachings advanced and asked him to use caution when he spoke of such issues.

Through Martha, Jesus felt the delicate knowing of the female world. When all is exposed in the light of truth, it will be revealed that Martha was the true balancing point that helped Jesus in focusing his light.

Jesus' Baby Sister, Ruth

Not so much an influence, but a beacon of light, was Jesus' baby sister, Ruth. Born shortly after their father Joseph's death, Ruth turned to Jesus to fill the fatherly role in her life. The blessings of this role are better understood when we remember that Jesus was here to experience all aspects of life, and it was with Ruth that he would experience the role of a father.

From the beginning, it was known that Ruth idolized her eldest brother. When it became time for Jesus to fully begin his ministry, his mother, as well as his brothers and sisters, felt some fear of abandonment each time he left home.

Ruth, however, never lost her great devotion to Jesus. It was her self-assumed duty to bring home to the family news of their elder brother Jesus' great quests. This was her way of encouraging the family to remain united. Her knowingness told her that it was her life plan to remain at home, where she was needed the most.

Eventually Ruth did follow Jesus on some of his travels. When she could not accompany Jesus, she would have him tell her over and over again, every detail of his trip. Some wondered why Ruth would ask Jesus to repeatedly tell the same stories. In truth, Ruth was offering a gift to the master by allowing him the opportunity to share his words of healing and love with the people.

It seemed that if anyone wished to gain an audience with Jesus, they would have to offer a good reason, or this young figure named Ruth would be found between the visitor and the master. Even the disciples hesitated to test her will, for they knew Ruth would see to Jesus' safety, to the point of throwing her body in front of the seeker if necessary.

On the day he was crucified, Ruth would be found at the foot of her brother Jesus' cross. She would witness the angels who were sent to escort the Christ Consciousness home to its Creator Light. As the Christ Consciousness left the body of the dying Jesus, Ruth's cry was so deep that Mother Earth felt her love. In that same moment, Ruth vowed that she would never allow the world to forget her brother's love for them. It is said that she cried from that moment on until Christ himself appeared to her, at which time he assured her that one day they would be together again.

Mary Magdalene

As for the women who surrounded Jesus outside his immediate family, there is one woman who was most notable, primarily because of the way other writers have portrayed her. That person is Mary Magdalene.

Readers of the Bible today have always found the stories of Mary Magdalene noteworthy. In the Biblical version of history, she is depicted as a prostitute or a lady of ill repute. In truth, when those who were responsible for the Bible saw how vast was her influence over Jesus, they felt a need to diminish the reputation of Mary Magdalene. They saw how much Mary Magdalene had taught Jesus about the world from a bigger perspective, and they depicted her in an adverse way.

Mary Magdalene's family history discloses not only how she was able to garner great quantities of information, but also why the writers of the Bible portrayed her with dishonor.

Mary was the daughter of the wealthy Magdalene family that owned and ran the port services of the Port of Magdalea. A busy port, Magdalea could offer ships a safe haven where they could obtain needed supplies to prepare for the next sea journey. When a ship of exploration entered port from faraway lands, it was the mandate of most port owners that the ship's logs or travel records had to be submitted to the port authorities. The logs were often written in great detail by the ship's captain and told of tremendous fortunes of the places they had visited. The logs described exotic-sounding lands that the ordinary human never dreamed existed.

Once the logs were turned over to the port authorities, they were meticulously copied. In most instances, the pilots or sea captains would then receive back the reproduced copies, and the originals remained with the port owner. Once again, as with the mystics and scribes, the knowledge gained from such records placed the readers of the journals on the same level with those who sat in seats of power.

Fortunately, Mary Magdalene was schooled at a very young age in the translation of these records. In this way, she could gain full access to learning of worlds beyond the common person's imagination. She spent much of her young adult life studying these records and gained insights that would ultimately help shape the world. Her retention of this information was said to be flawless because she had the gift of what would be considered today as "photographic memory."

Mary Magdalene would eventually share all this knowledge with Jesus. This information was far greater than that from so-called formal teachers who would ultimately try to cast disbelief on his work. In essence, Mary Magdalene gave Jesus the most modern conceptual education then available. They would spend long hours together, far into the night, going from one detail to the next of information Mary had garnered from the documents. This may explain why such a misconstrued picture would be painted of this female energy, Mary Magdalene.

Why was it of such vital importance that Mary Magdalene be thoroughly discredited? It is clear that she shared information with Jesus that was unknown to most at that time. Those surrounding Jesus, who recorded his life journey, had no way of claiming such knowledge to be truth. The men simply left much of the information out, primarily because Mary Magdalene was female and therefore, not held in the esteem of the rest of his followers. Eventually there would come a time when the males who did keep the records had to either admit she was right or discredit her by claiming her to be of evil ways. This would maintain the authority that those in power so diligently protected. If a woman, such as Mary Magdalene could have that much knowledge, how could the men possibly continue to keep the women in a subservient role?

Rebecca

Another truly misunderstood female energy in Jesus' life was the woman named Rebecca. She was a young woman who fell deeply in love with Jesus. She attempted to gain his love by using her father's great wealth as a lure. After presenting the needs of Jesus' family to her father, he offered to support Jesus' entire family. His love for his daughter was so great that he offered to pay for the education of Jesus and all of his brothers in areas that would best suit his own business.

When Jesus turned down this exceedingly generous offer, Rebecca was devastated. Jesus had known that in order to fully experience the role of being a father to his family, it had to be completed in the fashion he chose. This was a responsibility he held dear to his heart and he would not accept the influence of Rebecca's father's wealth.

It was only after Jesus fully revealed to Rebecca his mission on Earth that she understood why her efforts had been rejected. Eventually, Rebecca's love was so strong that she became one of Jesus' most ardent supporters in his later years.

Throughout the many journeys of Jesus and his disciples, Rebecca traveled ahead to greet them on their arrival, always making sure that their needs were well taken care of. As is often the case, those choosing to serve are usually the ones closest to the heart of the teacher. Such was the case with Rebecca who never sought monetary payment for her services. Instead, she lived only for the moments she would share alone with him, listening to his teachings.

On many occasions, Jesus asked Rebecca to accompany him to a place of solitude when he felt the need to separate himself from people who bombarded him with personal questions. Jesus and Rebecca sat together for hours, and she supported him while he worked through his journey on Earth. Never judging or trying to influence him, she was simply there for him. This was probably the closest relationship with a woman that Jesus allowed for himself. As for Rebecca, her devotion for this man was forever present.

The Eve of the Last Supper

Hidden deep within the lost scrolls exists a writing of Mary Magdalene which tells of the evening when Jesus called together his mother Mary, his Aunt Martha, and Mary Magdalene, herself. It was the evening prior to the Last Supper, when Jesus prepared for his departure from the earthly dimension.

On that night, Jesus entrusted these three women of his understanding of religion and the church. Jesus told them of the changes that would take place after his death. He wanted to forewarn the women of the difficult times they would face in trying to disseminate this information.

The conversations centered on how the world would ascend to a different level of responsibility if the church, in its growth, embraced the teachings of Jesus. He saw how the church had taken on a role of authority and how much of the teachings of the Creator had been lost. He saw how the masses were being led to believe in the separation of self from their Creator Light, and how the freedom of thought was being replaced by dogma.

Jesus revealed that he knew that his journey in this incarnation would be truly fulfilled. He clarified that he would be the light of the Creator's knowing, and in that he would be seen as a way to the Creator. This meant that his light would express the thought of the Creator on levels understandable by evolving societies, including the human world. His greatest desire for them after his departure would be to tell the world that he would serve as a master guide for their world until such time that they could remember the truth in its entirety.

The discussions of that long evening led also to the topic of the tenets of baptism. By that time, Jesus was fully conscious of his impending ascension back into Thought Light, where his journey with humanity would continue on. Although he fully agreed in the use of rituals in baptism, Jesus saw that the rituals themselves had to be changed. He clearly saw that the ritual of baptism needed to be experienced on a deeper level. Hence, Jesus instructed his three closest female supporters that baptisms thereafter be performed in his name, and in the name of the Christ Light, for he knew it would be well received in the Creator's Light.

Jesus reminded his listeners that it was time to ascend to a higher level of knowing. Each person who chose to become one in the Light of the Creator was, by standing before a human representative of this highest awareness in the rite of baptism, ascending into one's own light. When a person was baptized in the name of Jesus, one began a rite of passage into the limitless world of the All That Is. The person declared the knowing of Jesus' light and the connection to the mastery of his or her own awareness.

Jesus went on to say that upon receiving his light, those who would stand with this new light would be born to serve as radiant lights for others to see. Never would they need to call from the rooftops for others to join them. Rather, they would brighten their new light so that all who would see and feel the light would want to share their own inner peace.

To all of you who are waiting for the Christ Light to return to the Earth plane, you do so in vain. You cannot wait for something that is already here. You might want to look closely at where the idea of waiting for a reappearance of the Jesus presence began. Is it possible that this was originally established to curtail your direct interaction with this all-powerful light? I say, leave not your awareness bottled up in wishing and hoping for a return of Jesus, but simply let your heart show you the way.

After Jesus' Crucifixion

It is interesting to note that it was the three women, Jesus' mother, Mary, Martha, and Mary Magdalene, who first discovered the empty tomb following Jesus' crucifixion. When Jesus did appear for the first time following his crucifixion, he chose to appear before these three women. Was it because they just happened to be there, or was it because he felt safe in their presence? My friends, he chose to focus his energy only where true believers would be found. The women closest to Jesus were convinced he would return, for he had promised each of them that he would.

While the three women stood at the empty tomb, they tried to console each other. It is said that in their collective vision, there appeared before them a seemingly human energy form but without the density of a physical body. The form they beheld was more translucent, and as a voice emerged from this form, the Earth trembled.

Within moments, the three women recognized it was their beloved Jesus. What they saw was only an interim reality for his essence. This was truly difficult for them to understand. It was through pure love alone that Jesus helped them accept that his light had moved to a higher level.

Again, Jesus asked for the help of his mother, his Aunt Martha, and dear friend, Mary Magdalene. He requested that they find his disciples and gather them together for their final lesson plans, which he would deliver in human words.

The three women rushed about on Jesus' behalf, calling together the male disciples. It would not be an easy task to convince the disciples that Jesus was now in a higher awareness of light and that his choosing to manifest before them was an act of highest compassion. They were aware that fear would prevail among the men. Indeed, the disciples had scattered and gone into hiding following the last meal shared together with Jesus.

When the male disciples finally came together, they had a few minutes to await the arrival of Jesus. Even then did they question his light. How could it be possible that Jesus had died and was alive again? Was it really Jesus? Or were these women in such deep grief that they were seeing things?

The questions to the three women were endless. Then, in an instant, all who were there gathered began to feel the presence of Jesus. It was an energy so overpowering that each man fell to his knees in trepidation. They began to cry in tones never heard before. In their astonishment, the men became aware that the tones coming from their mouths were aligning the energy around Jesus, making him appear brighter and clearer to them. In their collective vision, they saw first the colors, then the clarity of his light body. Alarm spread amongst them, especially when they realized that Jesus was not touching the ground.

The truth of what they were experiencing suddenly became clear to all. They understood that the presence of their beloved Jesus was actualized by the emanations of light and sound that surrounded them. They had no further doubts. Instead, they rejoiced that their beloved Jesus had returned to them, just as he had said he would. Jesus had returned; he was alive. And now the whole of his light reality was brighter than ever. From that moment, they knew all of Jesus' teachings to be truth on a deeper level. They could now see the true closeness of the world of spirit.

Jesus' Final Message to His Female Disciples

After speaking with the male disciples, Jesus went on to meet with the female disciples. He told them of things he would be remembered for after his departure from their dimension. Through his energy alone, vibrating so fully, each could understand what he meant on many levels.

He explained to the women that the world was shifting, that the humans were grappling with this change. Although he had fulfilled his mission by sending forth his Christ Light throughout the world, the human population had not been ready to accept it. Even when the Christ Light was offered to them through Jesus, they chose to feel separation.

Separation was felt not only from each other, but from the Creator's Light as well.

As Jesus entered his energy into theirs, the women clearly saw that his mission was not about failure. It was his sole desire at that moment to allow all to become aware of a higher level of consciousness. This was his gift to humankind.

* * *

Questions and Answers:

Q: If Jesus were here to experience all of the five senses of the Third Dimension, did he ever have the desire for physical relations with a woman?

Kirael: That sounds like a question about sex. What a pleasure to expound on such a delicate state of awareness! Jesus did have feelings for the female world, possibly a bit more for some than others. Yet, it should be remembered that sex is one of many symbols of a shared love.

Over the years of evolution, the sexual act has taken on a life almost of its own. Most choose to see it as the illusion of attained levels of love, or more easily put, as the measure of one's love for another.

The master was so filled with love that by a simple touch, his energy would pass through another with a power few experienced. If this person was also resonating in love, the experience was said to be beyond description. As for the act itself, when one not only knows love, but also is love, no particular performance is necessary.

Q: Mary Magdalene and other female supporters had read in some records the existence of other people very similar in nature to Jesus. Were these people also aspects of the Christ Consciousness?

Kirael: What I'll expose here will likely be one of the more controversial points of this work. Remember that only those ready for change will be drawn to this writing.

In the infinite wisdom of the Creator, it is known that no one person or entity can change the consciousness of the human world. For that reason, the Creator allows for multiple entities to exist simultaneously to bring forth the healing energies to the planet.

The records that Mary Magdalene and others referred to did indeed speak of all-powerful entities that co-existed in different parts of the world. The records confirmed the existence of shamans and other grand beings that were known only to smaller groups of people. Each would receive an aspect of the Christ Consciousness and experience the human journey as Jesus did. It was their journey to be among the people and offer enlightenment to each person at their own level.

Wherever the Creator aligned an energy pattern to do the teaching, the entity would blend in perfectly. His speech would be consistent with those he was ministering to, and he was always trying to stretch the knowing of the masses. Many, like the Jesus entity, would encounter harsh and rigid belief systems and find it difficult to fulfill their roles. However, each shaman or grand teacher would do his or her best to awaken the people to the Creator's wisdom.

Each entity would focus on the level of awareness of the people they had come to share their knowledge with. For instance, there was an entity of the Christ energy that went amongst those who lived in what is now called the Americas. In this particular teaching, this shaman taught the people of how the Creator had orchestrated a delicate balance amongst the plant and animal kingdoms. And in the knowingness of the All That Is, the human world shall protect them.

Many of these masters were never documented in any books because there was little written language existing in most parts of the world in those times. Theirs was not to be remembered for what they had shared. It was for each of them on this Earth plane to bring to focus that no separation existed. All were of the same Light source.

Q: At the time of the crucifixion, or more precisely, at the moment of Jesus' death, it is said that a series of wails were heard that caused many at the scene to cover their ears. Can you explain why the wailing was so loud and intense?

Kirael: At the moment Jesus was released from his physical body, the women at his feet began to cry almost uncontrollably. They wailed from the feelings of intense separation. Then the light of the angel world overtook their energies. As this took place, the sounds of wailing were transformed. The sounds joined as one and became the same sound from which all life is patterned.

This means that when light particles come together to share an experience, like the women here, a sound is emitted. As each particle is drawn to this sound vibration, it takes on a more distinctive vibration. Each time something on this plane is brought into existence, a sound is produced to equal its light.

The sound formed by the women who were wailing at the foot of Jesus' cross was a combination of the resonance of Jesus being born back to the fullness of Christ and of the sound equating to evolution. In that moment, he was once again whole in the Creator's Light.

That which was emitted upon Jesus' death was like nothing ever heard before, or since. It was the sound within the light that resonates throughout all awareness. That same sound will only be heard when Christ implores the Creator to once again relieve the Earth of all fear, in what is called The Shift.

Q: Did Jesus have any particular healing techniques that he used?

Kirael: Jesus never really brought to the Earth plane a plan, so to speak, on how to heal. He didn't come here to teach a particular way. If you could have watched Jesus closely, you would have realized that the healings he performed took into account many different possibilities.

He healed with just his words alone. My friends, if you want to know the truth, his healing power was more with the word than it was with the touch. There were great throngs of people who gathered about him. And he spoke unto them, but usually only for a limited time because the crowds would normally crush him. Yet, in those moments of opportunity, he did speak words of healing unto them.

Crowds of people pushed forward and listened to every word that Jesus spoke. And believe me, my friends, there were vast, vast crowds—sometimes as many as three and four thousand would gather. You might be thinking that by today's standards that is not much, but in those days that was a large crowd. So Jesus would heal with the voice alone, and he would guide the people into their healing process.

Because Jesus had focused himself as human, he needed to utilize the words of humans. And in his openness with his God Creator, there was simplicity. There was never anything of great length, but only short little statements that created positive flows of energy.

Beyond that, he had many other ways of healing. There were times when Jesus would touch one person, putting the energy into that individual so that he might touch another. Jesus would take hold of someone in the crowd, and he would tell them to take hold of another. They would then pass the energy from one to the next until it would reach the one that he wanted to heal in the middle of the throng. And that person would be healed.

At other times, Jesus would just lovingly lay his hands upon a person. And there were two very important things that he would do. Always would he ask the person, "Is it your desire to heal?" Then he would listen for the answer, my friend. If he did not have the feeling inside, within his own love essence, that this person truly wanted to heal, he would immediately remove himself from that person, for he had learned not to interfere with a life plan. If someone had come into a space where he or she was diligently choosing illnesses of whatever kind, he allowed that person to live through that plan.

As for those, however, that came before him who had experienced all that they needed to experience from the illness, he laid his hands upon them and called to his Father. He would say, "God Creator, would you be so full of love that you would expend your energy within me— that I might ask the one who is to be healed to open unto my touch and allow the everlasting light to become a part of their reality? And thereby, send their journey into a new light, allowing for new and more beautiful spaces of opportunity?" For this is how Jesus spoke to the Creator with great reverence in his voice.

There are many statements made about Jesus on how he would open his light and shower it amongst the people. And there are those who would say that upon looking at Jesus, their eyes would burn. My friends, those who had to immediately shield their eyes from this light were notoriously those who were not ready to heal.

As healers during this Great Shift, you must recognize that many will come before you who do not believe that healing is possible. They have chosen a journey, and you may not interrupt that journey. You need only step back and offer them love until the moment they may choose for their healing to begin. You are not to judge, my friends. Jesus never judged. He just knew, and in that knowingness, all was healed.

6

Mastery: The Life Plan

Kirael's Numerology:
A "6" day reminds you that you are in control of your life. Leave
nothing undone. Complete all lessons. As master of your own life,
it is your great day to make masterful decisions and to ascend to
new levels of conscious awareness.

Author's Insights:

Whenever I travel and meet with people, questions arise about higher selves, soul mates, and soul families. Many have wondered about the consequences of an irreconcilable family conflict or the emotional scars of a distressing relationship. One common question is, Why is the human journey so difficult?

Early on, Kirael shared with me that energy patterns of light, such as guides and angels do not see our journey as difficult. They truly honor our human world. They might even appear envious of our opportunities to experience the levels of mastery. For while it may seem inconceivable to some, Kirael has often reminded me that we must wait for long periods of time before incarnating into the human reality.

Through Kirael as my teacher, my lessons have been vast. I have received an overview of how all developing life transforms from one reality to the next. Furthermore, what has come to light is that each human is working towards a mastery understanding of a single life plan. Each has the right to succeed.

In my knowingness, the answers we seek are available through the practice of meditation. If you can fully understand the magical journey called meditation, you will awaken to your own knowingness and mastery.

Kirael Speaks:

Let us consider the difference between how the human world sees the awakened state of meditation to be versus how the guidance world views it. First of all, when you consider yourself to be awake, we in the Guidance Reality see you as asleep. When you enter the state of non-physical energy motion, or the sleep state, we see you in your fully conscious or awakened state. In this awakened (while sleeping) state, you have the freedom to wander through the other dimensions and to experience the higher vibrational forces of the world that you have chosen to exist in. While you sleep, your higher self takes this opportunity to move your consciousness at its own will.

Conversely, when you master the art of meditation, you are able to direct the journey to attain varying degrees of awareness. The more you meditate, the better the end results. As with anyone first beginning a form of martial arts, you may feel awkward and only dream of what mastery must be like. Meditation is no different.

Have you noticed that beginners in martial arts sometimes dread going to practice? While they know the discipline is good for them, they still find themselves resisting the practice. Why is this? The answer is because they are embarking on a new journey in uncharted arenas. They are beginning an experience that is foreign to what they have previously undertaken.

It is a matter of being open to change. To achieve the desired result, you must realign many, if not all, of your systems. The body must be reoriented and stretched to new levels of flexibility. The mind must be open and receptive to interact with all this new input.

Above all, mastery of the martial arts involves emotions and understanding the emotional focus that is required. Without experiencing the emotional energy of the life journey, it would be difficult to attain any degree of success.

The same applies to the mastery of meditation. There are those who believe that the only form of meditation is sitting motionless for hours in a lotus position. However, you will find that the art of meditation goes beyond any prescribed technique. Like those in the martial arts, when one believes their technique is the only way to accomplish something, they usually find themselves on their backs in a defenseless position.

At this point, let me congratulate you if you are pretending to meditate. What do I mean by "pretending"? It's when you are sitting with a group of people in meditation and feeling that you are not getting anywhere with it. Believe it or not, you are.

By merely pretending to sit in a meditative state for approximately 30 minutes a day for 21 consecutive days, you still discover the truth of meditation. Every part of your journey is enhanced. You participate each day in loving yourself enough to experience all that is available.

The 10% / 90% Awareness

The brain of the human world is active on two distinctly separate dimensions of awareness. The first dimension of awareness is the less active 10% of the brain function. This part of the brain is responsible for gathering and storing information learned within this lifetime. Your five senses are constantly retrieving data and formulating it into sequential memory. Each entry is analyzed as it is received and set into motion, resulting in memory or action. When it is sent to the memory bank, each thought particle is categorically stored by its relevance to the situation it might be used for.

The other dimension of awareness, the 90%, is fully activated. It is in constant communication with the higher self and the All That Is. This 90% awareness of the brain functions as a receiver of information from a multitude of sources. As a rule, it will constantly absorb new levels of information and store away the data that do not resonate at the time for future interaction. It is constantly gathering knowledge that is not readily available in the matrix energy of the Third Dimension.

The question that often arises is how to move this information from the limited 10% awareness to the limitless possibilities of the 90%. The answer, my friends, is similar to what happens to my medium when he enters a "trans-state." In this state, he allows my energy to vibrate through him to be expressed as a conduit of my energy, at a level of consciousness acceptable by the human world. To do this, he must be willing to make adjustments in his 90% awareness.

Imagine that the 90% awareness of the brain is like a television set receiving waves of energy that carry signals. These signals turn into pictures and sounds when the television is turned on. Likewise, the 90% awareness constantly gathers information that can be used in the future. On another level, the energy waves create circulating energy patterns that result in stored vortexes of concentrated life-enhancing forces. These forces assist the humans in their evolutionary process.

Within the 90% awareness, you can clearly communicate with your guides and angels. You can also communicate with members of your soul family. For instance, my energy is in a constant stream of dialog with the 90% part of the medium's brain. Collectively, we are amassing knowledge in his file system that he uses, especially while traveling in his sleep state.

If the human species could access the full potential of the 90% awareness, all their questions would be answered instantaneously. They would have no reason to continue the journey. Perhaps this is why the human world holds their veils so tightly in place. With these veils, only the information that can be used in the Third Dimension is filtered into the processing part of the 10% awareness. It is in the 10% process that the human reality is limited by linear thoughts.

The 10% awareness of the brain continues to expand its energy as to facilitate the requirements of evolution. Neither does it truly rest. Although on a significantly lesser level than the 90%, the 10% is accumulating data even when the human body is in sleep state.

Transferring Energy from the 90% to the 10%

In some forms of meditation, you can reduce your brain waves to a minimal vibrational frequency. A transfer of information between the 90% and the 10% awareness can be accomplished through meditation. The 10% awareness aligns the particle transfer of information from the 90% into thought energy for you to delineate and understand on a third-dimensional level.

In meditation, your input by the 10% is less important, whereas the dialog between the 90% and your higher self is significant. This is because the higher self is always seeking to place its human energy self in the path of healing. This entails the higher self sending messages into the 90% portion of the brain in hopes that the 10% gets it.

The higher self knows that the first reading of this healing energy will be registered in the cellular awareness. When the cellular consciousness becomes aware that the higher self is sending it messages, the only thing that interrupts the flow is the 10% awareness that races through the system checking for data.

Slowing the interception of the 10% awareness through meditation allows for the higher self and the 90 % to communicate with the cellular awareness. In this way, the healing begins. The more often this occurs, the greater the interaction between the two parts of the brain. Hence, each meditation done to its fullest potential can be interpreted as a healing. Healing on the cellular level. Where better to begin a full healing journey than at the source?

The Levels of Consciousness

To help illustrate the levels of consciousness as it is "stepped down" within an evolutionary context, let me begin with the example below.

If you were to plug a radio directly into the power source at an electrical power plant, the influx of energy would burst the radio into a million pieces. The energy it takes to play this little appliance is infinitesimal compared to what is available at the source. This is why the power needs to be stepped down. The same applies when a light being chooses to vibrate at the human level. The energy is substantially stepped down to facilitate its incarnation.

In your own beginning stages of evolution, the light you chose to present as your expression of life force was aligned to an oversoul. This oversoul, which by design is beyond comprehension, is a mass of energy designated to perceive dimensional enlightenment on all possibilities. The oversoul is in direct relationship to the Creator and utilizes its current of particle light source to define itself.

Soul Families

The oversoul divides into units of energy that journey together into different dimensions. Each unit is known as a soul family. Each soul family is aligned to a specific purpose. Each purpose is determined by the level of awareness that the soul family has attained through multiple experiences. The number of members in a soul family is designed by evolutionary desire.

Within each soul family, members of all levels of soul age exist. There are young, medium and old souls in each family, thereby ensuring a balance of light. Each member goes through different experiences to enhance the learning of its collective family. Members of a soul family do not necessarily closely follow each other around through various incarnations. However, the possibility of meeting someone from your own family is not uncommon.

Higher Self

After the purpose of a soul family's journey has been established, it creates special patterns of energies, the higher selves, to gather lesson plans.

The higher self is one of the most complex parts of the evolutionary system. Each light being of a soul family registers its light to the source of incarnations through the higher self. Each higher self petitions the Creator to allow its incarnation into a life system best suited to enhance its total existence.

To carry out the lesson plans, the higher self maintains the ability to utilize all levels of awareness simultaneously. It extends its energy into whatever dimension it feels is necessary. This assures the highest level of awakening and the most thorough usage of vibrational body systems at all times.

You became human, my friend, to facilitate the evolutionary process of your higher self.

Higher Self Aspects

Once the higher self has begun the journey within the Creator's Light, it splinters its energy into magnetic formations of light and sound. Usually it divides itself into three separate vibrations referred to as "aspects." Each aspect or extension of the higher self then enters into the human embodiment to experience all the possibilities of the journey.

The soul purpose of each human aspect is to evolve in love with each incarnate opportunity it has on the Earth plane. Generally, each aspect is sent to separate, far-reaching areas of a particular planetary system because their energy, in close proximity, is detrimental to the cellular consciousness of the other.

The higher self may also establish aspects of itself on other planetary systems. When this occurs, it will usually be within systems that are interactive with each other. For this reason, humans will often hear of the star systems of Pleiades, Sirius and Andromeda. These star systems have what is known as "similar being status," which means they have lesson plans that are somewhat similar with yours. Although compatible, the level of vibrational advancement on these other systems is beyond the comprehension of what is referred to in other realities as the "Earth human's self-imposed five-sensory program analysis systems."

Walk-Ins

There are many cases in which the human soul energy has completed all it came to learn, and is ready to return to the Creator's Light while still having a highly functioning body system. In these situations, the higher self will enter a new aspect of itself into the perfectly healthy body. This new aspect will have a whole new set of lessons to learn that will amplify the evolution of its soul family.

Thus, if people awaken one day feeling as though they are someone different, they likely experienced an aspect transference, or a "walk-in." These processes can sometimes take months, even years, to complete. At other times it can happen overnight.

A walk-in transference can also occur during a traumatic incident, in which the physical body becomes so overwhelmed that it chooses to shutdown. What people might think is a coma could be the higher self that is transferring a new aspect into the body. When this occurs, the person has little memory of its past upon awakening from the coma.

There is another kind of walk-in which takes place when the higher self can no longer motivate its human aspect to evolve. For example, this occurs if a human vibration gets caught in a repetitive lesson and chooses to reenact its journey over and over. Then the higher self will place as many different possibilities as it can to break the spiral. If the spiral cannot be broken, the higher self has another option. The higher self can remove this non-evolving aspect of itself from the human embodiment and allow for an aspect of another higher self to use the body. This special transaction will further enhance the journey of the soul family.

The Critical Mass of Knowingness: "I Know"

The higher self allows you to achieve your lesson plans in whatever way necessary. You most likely want to know what your life lesson plans are first. Because your lesson plans notoriously escape your 10% awareness of the brain processing, I suggest that you first look at issues of work, family, money, relationships, or illness in your life. Recurring patterns of dissatisfaction in any of these areas are where your lesson plans exist.

You might say, " I have a back problem that just doesn't go away, but I've done all I can do to heal it." We in the Guidance Reality will respond by saying, "If you've done all you can do and your back problem persists, then you haven't done all that you can do."

I know that it is perplexing, yet I also know that the way to complete a lesson plan in totality is to search out what you still need to learn. When the lesson is not fully learned it is because you have missed something previously along the way. In a sense, you have left a stone unturned somewhere on the path.

Some of you are at the edge of the precipice, the critical point in your lesson plan. Instead of stepping off the precipice and seeking a new direction in your lesson plan, you hesitate and begin to create reasons to justify your incompletion. For whatever reason, you are unwilling to move forward. Possibly due to a lack of knowingness and fear, you are not able to complete your journey.

At this point, you need only to return to the pathway leading to the precipice. You notice stones that may have gone unrecognized before. Any one of those stones could be the one to realize your lesson plan in fullness. So you begin to look more carefully at each stone. With each stone, you realize the potential to enrich your journey. Yet, which is the stone to complete your journey?

By retracing your steps, you find the stone yet unturned. When you finally turn it over, you discover a tiny little spot on it. You say, "Oh, my goodness, was that it?" And yes, that was it! That was the missing part you needed to learn to complete your lesson plan in entirety.

Oftentimes, you look for major malfunctions in your life, when lo and behold, it is something of total simplicity.

"Well," you say, "this is so discouraging, Kirael. I keep returning down the path looking for that unturned stone and I can't seem to find it." Well, how badly do you want it? If you really want to learn the lesson, you will not mind returning again and again. Simply ask, "What did I miss? Guide me to find the stone that I have yet to uncover. Allow me to turn that stone over and experience the knowing."

This is your opportunity to use your 90% awareness on your path. By opening your heart to the Light of Creation in your prayers and meditations, you will gain the clarity on the steps to take to learn the lesson. The strength of your mastermind and your participation in your sleep state programming will expedite the learning process.

Completion comes when you have done everything you can to learn the lesson. It comes with your passion to heal. When you have turned over that last stone and learned the lesson offered, the lesson plan is complete. Then you can say, "I know" with such certainty that it is truly a state of knowingness. In that moment, you attain mastery.

Questions & Answers

Q: Why do I feel a closer affinity to my spiritual friends than I do to my own birth family?

Kirael: One day it will become clear that in the choosing of your birth parents, the degree of kinship is one of the least important factors brought into the equation. For instance, a soul may choose a parent based solely on the circumstances of location or belief systems.

Indeed, it should be remembered that there are no guarantees in any incarnation. You align the life lessons that you decide to complete in this lifetime, and then you have choices. The choices are made as close to perfection as one can get, yet the possibilities for error are quite high. This may be why you feel closer to your spiritual family than your birth family.

There are those reading this who have looked at their brothers and or sisters and wondered just how they got into the same family. Wonder no more, my friends; know that your true relatives, or the rest of your soul family, are out there looking at their relatives and wondering just like you.

Q: How can I remember what happened during my sleep state?

Kirael: While you sleep, many of you are traveling into other dimensions that have little resemblance to your Earth plane. Children normally wake up with a full recall of events during their night travel. Adults, on the other hand, usually do not. If you are fortunate enough to interact with energies such as the extra-terrestrials, you may gradually remember your sleep state journeys with them.

If you truly desire to remember your experiences in your sleep state, communicate to your higher self that you want to remain closer to the Earth plane during your sleep state. Your 10% awareness can interpret this information more readily. The best way to begin remembering your sleep state experiences is to place a pad and pen next to your bed. Upon awakening, write down all the facts you recall. Eventually, your writings will reflect the path you have been on during your sleep state.

Q: Why do we forget the agreements of our lesson plans?

Kirael: When you were home in the Creator's Light preparing for your incarnation on the Earth plane, you already knew everything that you wanted to experience. However, upon your arrival to the Third Dimension, you encountered the magnetic structure of gravity that pulled everything into a slowed-down version of reality.

Inconceivable as it may seem, you literally begged to get to the Earth plane so that you could slow everything down to experience it and watch it unfold. What you have forgotten is that everything vibrates so slowly that you forget from one moment to the next how they are related.

Q: Do you have any suggestions on how I can communicate with my guardian angels?

Kirael: Opening a wave of communication with your higher self and other unseen forces of light is much easier than most would believe. Any light force that is designated to be accessible to the human world is virtually ready to assist at all times. But first, it must be remembered that very few forces of light are restricted by the illusion of time. We, in the Guidance Realm do not have any need for sleep. Thus, we maintain a constant awareness of all that is part of our reality. Our capability to interact with multiple experiences is unlimited, and the same applies to the interactions with the angels.

Let us explain the communication skills needed to interact with the angelic light force. It is quite the same as listening to the higher vibration of the self.

Firstly, let me emphasize that angels do not have vocal cords. Therefore, it does not make sense to expect them to speak to you in a resounding voice. Know that angels can and do interject thoughts into your reasoning and deductive systems without the use of vocal vibrations. If you meditate in earnest, you will perceive their thoughts. Their response is in direct proportion to your desire to allow them to be of service.

Secondly, by posing the question to the angels in clarity and with passion, you will receive their response immediately. For the most part, angels will not respond when your questions are clouded by random thoughts.

The wave of communication with angels is the easiest form of communication available to the human vibration. It works on all levels of awareness—with your higher self, angels, guides, or for that matter, those you refer to as extra-terrestrials. All you need to do is listen.

Q: I am interested in channeling. Could you please explain the process involved in being a transmedium?

Kirael: It would be my pleasure to describe the varying degrees that you can reach in your desire to interact with the unseen forces of light.

First, I would like to state that the rarely used 90% awareness portion of the human brain is a receiver for all input. This includes input from all levels of awareness, including the light forces in the worlds of your dolphins and whales. When they wish to communicate their desires and/or assistance towards the humans, they use sound vibrations that resonate within the human's 90% awareness.

So imagine, if you will, a portal which appears to be a cylindrical column of energy that extends from your 90% brain sensors into your 10%. If you are uncertain in your desire to hear what is being transmitted, the walls of this portal appear thin and porous. When this is the case, your third-dimensional thought processes lessen the possibility of clear communication. Your doubts and fears interfere with the transmissions, and thereby taint the information that you receive.

the portal becoming thicker and more solid. Imagine that by strengthening the walls, the energy passed through it takes on stronger levels of clarity as well.

Next, create a second portal surrounding the first one. Then, in the space between the two portals, imagine a layer of matrix numbers that prevent any third-dimensional thoughts from entering in. The defined walls of the portals maintain a column, whereby my conceptual thoughts can pass through and vibrate directly to the vocal cords of the medium. This, in simple terms, is what is involved in transmediumship.

An example of one who has learned to do this is the person whom I call my medium, Fred Sterling. He has chosen to establish the foremost vibration in portal passages to allow my essence to speak directly to those in attendance. Please know that in order for my communications to be transmitted successfully, there must be as little stress on the medium as possible. To maintain our relationship, he must feel secure that our journey is compatible for both the listener and his energy. It is by choice, therefore, that I do not stretch the bounds of his language or belief systems to a point where he loses the ability to function in his chosen energy pattern.

This is why we from the Guidance Reality choose extremely carefully the mediums through which to deliver our messages. We do not choose humans with limited awareness to further the light of awareness. In truth, they are predestined connections.

7

Transition: Healing in Truth, Trust, and Passion

Kirael's Numerology:
A "7" day signals that it is time to move on. A day of great
awareness, you can experience the day on multiple levels
simultaneously and move from one level to the next. You are in the
flow of change and transformation.

Author's Insights:

There can never be too many people searching for new, more unifying healing techniques. The need for an integrative system that heals on all four levels of awareness (physical, emotional, mental, and spiritual) will find practitioners moving beyond the boundaries of their discipline. This evolution will create the highest potential of complementary care.

The world is changing, and we need to respond to those changes. We must transition from the world of the bystander to one of proactive caring. This will take as many healers as there are those needing to be healed. It is my belief that with preparation, everyone can take an active role in the healing process.

The healing modalities can vary from healer to healer, yet all have similar desired results. Whether it is an ancient form of healing or one of the many new theories available, the utmost importance is to awaken to a higher state of consciousness. This happens on many different levels through the activation of healing energy that is brought forth in love. Embracing the Shift through the healing world will allow humanity to understand the totality of the God Creator essence. We will awaken to the Light of Creation within the self through the interaction of our five sensory experience and with the addition of our sixth sense.

Kirael Speaks:

When your higher self decided to enter an aspect of light called human onto the Earth plane, you came with a life plan to learn a number of lessons. If your plan included a lesson involving genetic diseases, then that was something you wanted to experience in that lifetime. However, because of the energy of the Shift, you no longer need to live out the lesson plan of having a genetic disease. Instead, you may wish to expand that lesson by learning how to heal that disease.

That is what the Shift is about. The Shift is to teach everyone that the human world can change. It is about knowingness, and loving yourself enough to want to heal, for there is absolutely nothing on the human journey that cannot be healed.

We in the Guidance Realm wish to open a space where the mastery of healing is revealed to anyone who desires to participate. It begins with three basic principles in the world of healing that always lead to miraculous results when practiced.

The Freedom of Truth

First, there is the principle that all healing must be held in Truth within the trinity of Truth, Trust, and Passion. This applies in any situation and on any level of conscious awareness to bring a person to complete healing. It means that truth in healing must be expressed in the fullness of love. The person being healed must experience every level within the healing process. If not, the illness will simply find another way to manifest at a later time. The healer is there only to assist in the journey.

Even Jesus, one of the most beloved healers to experience the human journey, had to remember that it was not his mission to heal people beyond their chosen journeys. A story is told of Jesus following his baptism. It involved a healing of such monumental importance to him that he felt compelled to have Peter, his disciple, record the event word for word.

Peter Transcribes

Jesus addressed Peter by saying, "My friend, please take each word into your heart as you make a record of this message. Scribe for me the following words so that it may be remembered that only the Father Light has the awareness to alter a human journey.

"To allow one in this life to alter another's journey is the same as imposing thy will within a life that is not present of soul. To master the light of healing, it must be held truth that it is the will of the person presented to thee that releases the limits and sets the level of healing to be accomplished.

"In my beginning encounters of healing with the essence of human, a child of great blemish did approach me. As I gazed upon her, my eyes held the pain in her being. My heart opened to the desire that I may mend completely all of her wounds. Without approach to the world of my Father, I bent to her, laying my hands upon her head and called forth my full awareness of love to banish these scars of her life that outwardly were long past ready to be vanished.

"In an immediate unfolding of events, her life light was altered under my touch. Her skin beheld the look of youth, while her body trembled in spasm. I myself was thrown into a world of light never witnessed before. It was as though the whole of the world missed a stroke, and we both transcended into this force of light. Mine own force was moved to soaring beyond the light of this earthly world.

"I found myself in the total grace of my Father's Light, and I knew in that instant that I was holding the Light within my entire being. I stood within a power unfelt in all my earlier experiences. I felt fortuned to experience and hear the presence of this all-powerful knowing. Though no words of language were spoken, it was without doubt that all was heard in the greatest of clarity.

"I was led to speak to the overlife of this little girl whose life had just been altered. Though this power spoke in great love, it would be clear that what had happened should be seen in the full light of awareness.

"It told of the journey of its human part of self, the girl. It allowed my light to witness the chosen plight of her life journey. She had come to this world as a lesson for the masses to acknowledge her humanity without pity. Clearly the force of a full restoration of healing in the physical world would be done at a pace best aligned to all that would interact with her.

"As I came upon her, her journey had not yet unfolded. The moment she was enveloped in mine own charge, she was taken to a level of healing which no longer allowed her to remain on her committed journey in the Light of the Father.

"In short, in my zealous haste to deliver this human light to a space of freedom from her woes, and in my simple judgement responding to her appeal to me for healing, I failed to remember that each comes to the path of knowing in one's own measure. The overlife power allowed it to be seen that never should I move such energy to ensure a gift of life, nor should light be altered to amend the grace of another. Always must we allow each to unfold to the journey of choice.

"When a person comes to the divide in his or her journey, thereby allowing for healing, only then shall we present ourselves. Even in this light shall we bring energy unto the level best used in the total journey. In my haste to present this small child to the power of the Father, desiring that she may accomplish her destiny without peril, I alone had committed her to the light of an altered life.

"Heed this: We all follow the plan of each human we are called upon to heal. In this are we complete in the spiral of their choice. When we know of the whole plan, allow us to surrender to the path of our Father that the will of each soul is done."

These words of Jesus, spoken in the energy of the Christ Light, should remind all that only the Creator may alter a life plan. This should be a reminder to all that in the journey of human, each is entitled to choose whichever path is best suited to the desired outcome.

Those who choose to be in the role of healer as true masters must follow the rules of truth. In this, all plans are revealed. The true healer knows that the person seeking healing must exercise his or her choice of freedom. Then when the light is such that the person is ready to move past the physical manifestation, without exception, the healing of the body is possible. Looking for an instant cure may lead to disappointment, for in reality, it may be the person's journey to experience this particular healing on all levels. It may be that only by completing the healing on each level will total physical healing be ensured.

The healer must never lose faith. Guidance on the healing process is often needed. If it is the will of the person to complete the healing on all levels, it is in the power of the healer to keep the light lit. At that point, it is only a matter of time before the desired result manifests. Bask not in wonderment of the outcome, bask only in the amount of love used to complete the mission.

The Art of Trust

The second component of healing is the modality of Trust. The word in itself creates a space where many will experience fear. The reason is most people who have placed their trust in another's plan have almost always found pain and disillusionment in the end. It is likely that some of you reading this work are in fear of surrendering to a love with someone else. You are afraid to feel the pain should something go awry, while others of you do not trust yourselves to ask for what you want because you cannot deal with rejection. Most humans do not trust because that would require trusting in the higher power of love.

Trusting in the Creator is one of the greatest tests of the healer, particularly in the most acute levels of the healing journey. During these times, true healers understand the importance of trusting the Creator. They find that when they trust all of life essence, they have tapped into the life force of the Creator. Then they realize that they are conduits of the life force of the All That Is.

Healers must trust that when they are working with others on healing, they are doing part of their own journey. This leads to the best possible outcome for both involved. By choosing to live within the space of truth and trusting in a power not fully understood on this plane, the healing shifts into full completion.

The Essence of Passion

The most difficult to explain, yet by far the simplest part to enact, is the third modality of healing: Passion. This is the direct alignment with the Creator's energy. When humans discover the true essence of passion, they experience the love they came to the Earth plane to understand. In the absence of passion, complete healing does not occur.

In healing, one might measure the level of commitment to the process of healing by the passion they emanate. For the healer to attain the expression of passion, an alignment of conscious awareness involving all four bodies (physical, emotional, mental, and spiritual) must be completed. This again is only possible when the healer and the one being healed are brought together in Truth, Trust, and Passion. Such an alignment allows for the healing to unfold with little, if any, linear thought. Both people are truly in the flow of healing, and the world around them disappears into enlightened awareness. On this level, healing has reached the state of grace where one realizes that there are no limits to the possibilities being sought.

The word "passion" should never be misconstrued with intense physical pleasure. These are two separate energies. When the physical body aligns with pleasure, the feeling can be described by the five senses, whereas when the entire being is in a state of rapture, the unity of the whole is enjoined with the passion of the All That Is.

The Life of an Illness

As with the human journey, an illness has a birth, life, and death. It is designed to accomplish a certain set of lessons and goes to whatever lengths needed to complete its lesson plan. Until the lesson is completed, the life of the illness exists within the cellular consciousness of the person.

So let us look at the human body as a symphony orchestra with many instruments playing together. When one part plays off-key, the resultant sound reflects the discordant energy. To restore harmony, the discord is searched out and corrected. Thus, like the orchestra, harmony is perpetuated within the body when each part is willing to participate in a symphony of cellular consciousness. This occurs when there is a merging of cellular awareness in total alignment with all surrounding universal energies.

Until then, the core essence of an illness has its own set of fears, much like humans have. The illness has as much fear of losing its life as you humans have. It has a mission and wants nothing more than the opportunity to complete its mission. It does not see its energy as something evil; it sees it as an intricate part of the symphony that is being played out in the human body. If you view an illness in this manner, you begin to understand why it chose to be a part of the journey and how it will return to the light. Then the results will be nothing less than miraculous.

Take for example a person who is working with a tumor. The tumor can be recognized as having a life force of its own. Knowing the source of the tumor allows the healing to occur at a quicker pace. Understanding why the tumor has manifested rather than focusing on the worst possible outcomes, it no longer needs to exist. Becoming clear on whether the tumor is part of the current life lesson or of an unresolved past life permits a multitude of journeys to be dealt with at the same time.

At times, complacency sets in and a person may no longer wish to discover all the lessons offered within the healing journey. This creates a spiraling set of lessons. These spirals are the repetitious energies that collect when one is in denial of the life situation being experienced, or when the situation is not dealt with in a thorough manner. The spiral then begins to replicate its force over and over, continuing to resurface in one's life until the lessons are fully experienced.

From the human perspective, everything on the Earth plane may appear at times to be disconnected from the total. Each human may feel separated from the Creator force that holds this entire process together. For many, it may seem as though each human is alone on a chaotic journey of never-ending lessons that appear as one problem after another. However, nothing, my friends, could be farther from the truth. The truth is that the "essence" of all beings exists simultaneously on multiple levels.

The Journey of an Illness

The journey of an illness is a four-body experience. It begins to unfold when a vibration in the spiritual body is out of alignment with the Creator's Light. If healing does not occur, the higher self sends the discordant energy from the spiritual body into the next closest vibration, called the mental body or the thought system. However, if it gets lost in the confusion of the mental body it will move to the next available body of energy, known as the emotional body. The emotional body is the most energetically charged of the four bodies. If the lesson is still not learned, it automatically moves into the only space left to manifest in, the physical body.

Without fail, a lesson plan that has not been dealt with in the first three energy bodies will come to light in the form of a dis-eased cellular vibration of the physical body. The origination of the dis-ease must then be defined in order for the healer and the person to be healed to create a plan that will reset the vibration of the physical self.

Whether one suffers from a sore throat, or from life altering forms of cancer, the determining factor depends on the severity of the lesson plan to be learned. No matter the depth of the issues, healing can prevail.

It might be well to remember that illness must be fully experienced now. Lesson plans involving long, progressive illnesses will not be available in the Fourth Dimension. This is why so many are using this current lifetime to endure cancer, AIDS, and many other life-threatening diseases. Such illnesses will not be found anywhere except the first level of the Fourth Dimension. Even then, the experience will be reduced to such a degree that the opportunities to understand the depth of the lesson are minimal.

Seven Levels of Awareness

The stage of evolution you are presently at will determine your entry level in the Fourth Dimension. A brief look into the seven levels will explain the importance of moving through your lesson plans at a quickened pace. Remember, each of you must do the journey of healing.

Do not look at these levels as absolutes, but as levels of potential growth. View each one as a projection of the Creator's Light, and in this, you will see the perfection of each level.

Level One

Level One is reserved for those who have made a commitment to move into the fourth-dimensional energies. They are at Level One because they have not yet fully experienced the lesson plans set in place by their higher selves. Level One utilizes holographic imagery on a highly activated awareness level for those who need to go through certain experiences. In essence, that which you fear most will be manifested within a hologram, and once the fear is experienced within the hologram, that part of the lesson plan is completed.

You will want to avoid this level as much as possible.

Level Two

Level Two is the equivalent of the schoolhouse that Mother Earth and her inhabitants have been working on for thousands of years, with one exception. All plans that were being worked through on the Third Dimension are accelerated on Level Two. They are processed through the comprehensive matrix alignment systems of this level. Seemingly, the 10% awareness portion of the brain is initiated into the 90% awareness of the brain functions thereby eliminating the limitations of duality. On Level Two, you transition into the trinity consciousness. The pace of understanding is so fast that you will utilize the higher light energies of this level to bring closure to any incompleted plans.

Level Three

Level Three is for those who have the awareness to evolve, but who still have not embraced the truth of spirituality. Much of the Earth's population will begin their journey at this level. Each lesson will be experienced on an individual basis. Each possibility will be contained within a trinity element so that the full lesson can be seen on multiple levels simultaneously. At Level Three, you will experience the trinity of the Creator's Force, i.e., Truth, Trust, and Passion. You will be allowed to see many of the great masters in their teaching roles.

Level Four

Level Four is the most expression-filled of all the levels. This is where lessons mastered in the past are now brought to heightened states of interaction. Whereas previously you only discovered other realities through dreams and meditations, here you can use de-molecularization to move your energy from one place to another. The art of dream traveling takes on a whole new reality. Visions can be drawn into magnetic vibration, thereby offering you the possibility of experiencing your manifestation. If there were a place you might have conceived as heaven, Level Four will be as close to it as you can get.

Level Five

You attain a mastery comprehension of all living force at Level Five. Love simply is, and for this, it needs no explanation. The life force is in motion. No limitations to evolutionary perception remain at this level. All comes to clarity in the exact moment you speak the words.

At Level Five, each acts within a collective consciousness to initiate energy collaboration. Those choosing to manifest illusions will receive guidance, the first of which affirms that love has no opposite. This is a challenge for the human 10% awareness because of your use of linear thought.

Level Six

This is where the collective force of reality reaches the Nirvana of enlightenment. The All That Is becomes the "All At Will," and in this, only the "I Know" exists. Mastery is the only understanding one vibrates in.

Level Seven

Many of you may be thinking that when you reach Level Seven, you have reached the height of the Fourth Dimension. Instead, Level Seven is the experience of transition. Here, you live in cohesive awareness with all life forms. Indeed, you will most likely choose to vibrate in the world of mastery on multiple levels simultaneously. For instance, you could experience being a master guide living in the Angelic Realm, while playing an important role in the human awareness. Each is aligned into the All That Is. Each takes on various vibrational roles of the Creator while no longer having a defined essence. The journey into all levels of awareness is endless.

Questions and Answers

Q: To achieve healing on the highest level, you have stated that the alignment of Truth, Trust, and Passion between the healer and the person seeking healing is very important. If I am a person seeking healing in a typical medical setting where I hardly know my doctor, what do you suggest I do?

Kirael: Become quite demanding, my friend. If you have learned anything from this work at all, let it be that "the journey" is the all-important factor in any healing. The healing journey involves you taking your doctor to new heights of clarity in his explanations of your healing process. Do not leave your doctor's presence until you totally understand what is to take place. Your insistence on the doctor's focus on clarity will naturally lead to more precise forms of treatment for you.

Your physician will most likely focus on one aspect of the healing process, the physical body. As you continue to ask questions, your physician will become aware that your healing journey exists on the emotional, mental, and spiritual levels as well.

Do not surrender to what is convenient for the medical system. Your healing is your life's journey, so don't allow for any shortcuts. If the answers you receive are insufficient, then immediately search out an alternative healer to help support you in your healing process. Naturally, this is not to replace one for the other, but to complement the process.

When a person visits my medium for healing, he is willing to discuss every aspect of the healing journey that the two will participate in. As he explains the different levels they will likely experience, a bond begins to develop. The clarity on how each will participate in the healing process contributes to the desired outcome.

Q: Sometimes I feel that my inability to trust the healing journey prevents me from healing at the deepest levels, which means I might repeat the illness. How do I heal my issues of trust?

Kirael: The answer, my friend, lies in the knowing that you are part of a beautifully laid out plan called life. No one answer fits all. Yet, it might best be said that trust comes from constantly pressing forward. When one holds open the possibility that anything can happen, the need to keep trying will push you beyond the limits set within the human world. Never quitting will open new avenues to complete the journey at hand.

If the ultimate plan of your healing is to experience the death process and you decide to allow for this, you will still want to experience every possible part of the process. In that way, the journey is completed to its fullest extent.

Q: How do I begin to heal my fears that have veiled my cellular consciousness?

Kirael: Within each human embodiment is what we call the "Signature Cell" that holds a particle of light from the God Creator.

This is the cell that resides in the pineal gland. It is the cell that knows only perfection; the cell that begins the whole process.

When you decide to incarnate in the Third Dimension, the signature cell carries within it the vibrational light energy of your life plan in perfection. As the rest of the cells are developed to create the entire body, each of the cells begins its own memory program: where it belongs in the body, how to replicate itself, and all the other things that the cell must do.

As feelings of fear begin to veil the cellular understanding, your physical body may develop illnesses to call your attention to the healing process. You think, well, if I really want to heal, then I'll just think positive. This however is not always enough to cure the total ills of the four-body system. Positive mental attitude is one part of the healing, but oftentimes the healing needs to focus on a deeper level.

So you ask, How do I get in touch with my fears below the so-called veils? How do I begin to heal the cellular consciousness of my body?

Well, there is a way to get below the thought consciousness of the mind, and to the source of the dis-ease, through the vibrational patterns of sound and light. Through the touch of another human being, an energy pattern of sound and light is created and directed to the signature cell within the pineal gland. As you pass that energy through the gland, the process awakens the cellular consciousness of the dis-eased cells to its perfection. There's so much more to this topic, but that's for the next book.

Suddenly, things in your life begin to change. You receive both subtle and direct insights on how to support your healing process. For example, you may experience a burning desire to do more exercise, or to communicate with a loved one, or to receive a healing.

Essentially, your cellular consciousness is letting you know what it needs. If you ignore the insight, it is because the 10% awareness of your brain is still working with the dis-ease, while the cellular memory is working with the perfection of healing. You can amplify the perfection of the healing process through prayer and meditation, prana breathing, and by saying to yourself, "I love myself enough to heal."

Q: How important is prayer in healing?

Kirael: Without this question, this work would be incomplete.

Much of your life is spent asking for something from somebody. In the literal sense, even prayer is about asking. Prayer is the asking for clarity. In prayer, you slow your thoughts down. This opens a space where your mind can shift gears and allows the answers to be heard.

One process the human world would do well to remember is first to ask, then to remain quiet enough to hear the answers of the angels and guides. All powers of light are willing to be of service. When asked to guide a human, they will do so without fail. Not only do they want to help, but it is their life purpose to do so. If guides and angels could experience frustration, it would be listening to the thoughts of humans, then watching as they moved directly onto another thought without waiting for the answer.

Ask for guidance by formulating the most understandable question, and then listen. The angels and guides will communicate with you by placing thoughts in your mind. The moment the last word of your query is expressed, the answer begins. So stop thinking that you are not getting it, and just listen. You will be surprised.

Q: I am interested in reducing my weight by following a healthier diet, but I don't know where to begin. How can I find the right diet for me?

Kirael: At times, my answers are so simple that the person asking the question will ignore them because, by third-dimensional thinking, nothing can be that easy.

The most effective way to reach that perfect weight will be through a constant diet of prayer and meditation. All the diets on the market will be unsuccessful until you are totally clear on why you want to lose weight.

Weight loss is actually a healing process, and the need for a healer is essential. Together with the healer, you can establish a plan that will create the desired results without any frustration or stress in the process. This will be discussed at great length in our new healing book.

Q: The ultimate transition is called death. Is there a way of looking at this without fear?

Kirael: First, you might consider just how many deaths the average human experiences in a single incarnation. If you accept the changing of personalities as death, most of you die just about every seven years.

Each time your higher self feels that its current vibration has learned all that is possible at a given level of awareness, it begins a methodical clearing of the present energy. It initiates new levels of learning possibilities. Sometimes these are somewhat minor; at other times, they are quite extensive. This happens on average every seven years.

It is commonly known that both female and male incarnations live very defined lives. Females will usually terminate one life awareness and begin a new life around the age of forty-two. Males do this at age forty-nine. Now don't hold me to exact ages, for it can happen anywhere within a year or so of the ages mentioned. Yet, if you are, or know someone around that age, take a closer look, and you will see the changes. Or if you have already passed that stage, think back and take another look. Most of you will have entered new careers or gone through some life-altering experience around that age. This is especially true for lightworkers.

The ultimate experience of evolution is referred to as death. But actually, it would probably be more accurately stated the other way around, that when one prepares to leave this plane of awareness, it should be called "birth." In a sense, death could be called the ultimate experience of freedom. When one has completed all, or as much as possible in this plane of existence, they elevate their awareness to the next phase of learning. (Refer to *Kirael: The Great Shift* about suicides, so as not to make any mistakes about that journey.)

To take it one step further, you will enter into a life review immediately following the death transition. In the life review, you will see what has been completed and decide how much longer you will remain at that particular level. If there are third-dimensional lessons still unlearned, the process of reincarnating must be agreed upon by all levels of consciousness, including the Creator.

Soon all will view the death experience in its truest light. Death will not be seen as the opposite of life or as a journey being terminated. It will be understood that death is a point of transition. It will involve seeing clearly the illusions of life incarnations and the possibilities that exist beyond the confinements of the physical body.

It is truly a wonderful journey that awaits all who choose to use incarnations to evolve their energy. Be thankful that vibrational space has been available for your light, so that you could experience one of the most sought after journeys in the universe.

Q: I wish to enter into the Fourth Dimension at Level Four. What can I do now to transition into that beautiful space?

Kirael: "Learn the lessons." I imagine these words will not be sufficient as a complete answer. Yet, my friend, little else could be done in its place.

To arrive at such a level, most of the third-dimensional lessons in duality must have been embraced in knowingness. To arrive at a complete knowing of anything, you must have reached a full understanding of the physical, emotional, mental, and spiritual levels.

Do not get discouraged. Just keep moving forward at a brisk pace and never look back. Continue to learn as though your "level" in the Fourth Dimension depended on it.

8

Infinity: Traveling Between the Worlds

Kirael's Numerology:
An "8" day signifies that the present is being shared in two realities
at the same time, as in a loop. You are in simultaneous connection
with both spirit and matrix energies. If you can remain in the center
of the loop looking out at both directions, you are in a good space.

Author's Insights:

I magine feeling out of place most of your life, then awakening one day to learn that you are of galactic origins. A friend of mine has no childhood memory, except for looking up into the sky endless times and wondering if he was from somewhere out there. Can you imagine his relief upon learning from Kirael that he was indeed of galactic origins, and that he was on Earth to fulfill a mission?

Many of these beings have incarnated into human form to play a part in the Shift. Their sender units created such perfectly formatted ego systems that they forgot their galactic origins almost immediately upon incarnating on the Earth plane. Now that the energy of the Shift is taking such a toll on the magnetic pull of Earth, however, many are remembering that they really are not from this planet.

Hopefully, by reading this chapter, you may discover that extra-terrestrials are our galactic brothers and sisters. In that context, I share with you my first interactions with a new friend, a galactic being of extremely high mental telepathic powers.

It Begins

As I entered into meditation one evening, I became acutely aware of a presence that was shrouded from my direct view. Since this was not the first time, I was ready to interact with it, as long as it was of the Light.

I was aware that this energy was observing me without attempting to intercede, so I ignored it and drifted into the familiar feeling of my sleep state.

Abruptly, and without any warning, I was pulled forward and propelled into deep space at lightning speed. I checked to see if I was breathing. To my alarm, I realized that if I was, it was not apparent to me.

Suddenly, I was immersed in a light so brilliant that I tried to close my eyes. I must admit I felt fear. At the same time, I found myself switching to a mental organizer, without having the slightest idea of what it was.

Our First Meeting

In a space of non-existent time, I became aware of the same presence that had been in my meditation earlier. I found myself approaching a being that stood slightly taller than an average-sized human. This being of a female orientation was so luminous that I would describe her as electrifyingly beautiful.

The two of us studied each other for a time. I looked at her with curiosity, while she seemed to regard me as someone from her distant, yet warmly remembered past.

I gradually began to hear harmonic sounds. They were word forms coming directly from this female entity. While they continued to engulf me, her mouth remained motionless. By listening carefully, the sounds became more audible and I began to understand the series of tones that were being related. It was apparent that the beginnings of communication were possible between us.

This first encounter began with absolutely no formalities. She explained that she had communicated with Kirael. I noted the reverence with which she spoke Kirael's name and that she referred to him as "Master" Kirael. Knowing this helped me relax more.

I realized that I was there to learn about beings from other realities. More specifically, I was there to learn about our friends of the galactic realities. From the way she described the hierarchy of the ET world, I sensed that this beautiful being of light was of an advanced awareness.

In her presence, I felt like a kindergarten student.

She finally identified herself as Tara and explained that she was my host on this other-dimensional journey. She made it known that she was a direct descendent of one of the Guardians of Developmental Societies. Tara shared that she had incarnated on over one hundred civilized planetary systems, including a lifetime on Earth prior to the lifetime of Jesus. She also shared much about the ancient Lemurian and Asian cultures.

Her original vibration in Earth measurements was approximately 900 billion miles away from planet Earth, or about 150 Light Years away. Tara must have read my thoughts about this when she interrupted mine with, "It's much closer than you think."

Imagine an entity filtering through your thoughts, the thoughts of your entire lifetime. It was as though she was scanning my brain file system, unsure of where to begin her lesson on galactic entities. She finally looked deep into my eyes, and I am sure she said, "At the beginning."

I pride myself in dealing confidently with different realities, but I knew then that I was out of my league. While searching for ways to save my earthly dignity, I realized that my host was also in communication with my higher self, as if I was not present. She assured my higher self that a great alignment could be formed with its human component, me. I guess that was supposed to make me feel better.

Then right in the midst of an earthly fit of ego-driven thinking, I found myself engulfed in the gentlest of energies. Kirael had just interceded. He told her that if I were not treated kindly, he would take over the teaching. That would mean Tara would become the student for the third time. This must have held great significance to Tara because I suddenly became Tara's long lost friend. To my relief, the nightlong experience that had started off on shaky ground was rapidly moving to greater levels of awareness.

Speaking in the Now

Tara proceeded to explain that she was from a galaxy just outside the Milky Way Galaxy. The sun in the solar system of her essence guardian had at one time been almost five times larger than our sun. But after great periods of time, that sun had shrunk to approximately the same size as ours.

Tara reminded me that every thought I had was simultaneously processed in the "quadulactic" (don't run for your dictionary) layers of her "frontal lobe presence recorder." She must have sensed my dismay in my inability to grasp her explanation, so she offered a parallel energy thought through an analogy of the dolphins. If I would just remember how the dolphins communicated, her recorder would make sense, she said.

Then she switched to another topic. Tara spoke of evolutionary systems, explaining that all evolutionary systems are functioning in a retardant manner. In essence, the magnetic resolve of every evolutionary system is waning from the very beginning. The existence of the Third Dimension is limited in the same way due to diminishing magnetic energy fields.

As my mind pondered that, she explained that our planet had been chosen to reformat its energy into a higher vibrational sequencing. This would allow humans to move into the Fourth Dimension, where the sixth sense energy plays a prominent role.

At the same time, I was being shown the actual codes of vibration that brought the current Earth matrix into existence. I realized that Tara was showing me the blueprints of the system of the third-dimensional matrix. The architects of planet Earth, I learned, still held the formula of conversion to adjust the frequencies of the mainframe systematic converters. She said that the architects would wait to make the frequency adjustments until just before the Shift. This would ensure non-intervention of the galactic worlds until the human population was ready to interact with them.

My brain smoldered with so much information being received on so many levels. It was as though I was on hyperdrive and my brain was in overload.

A Healing Space

Sensing that my mind was wandering, Tara began to emit sparkling light particles in my direction. This immediately caught my attention, and I found myself drawn into their midst. I seemed to be getting lightheaded. I was definitely losing my ability to focus.

As quickly as it started, this sensation subsided. I found myself in a sterile surrounding much like a hospital. As my focus grew clearer, I found Tara to my right. To my left was another, much larger being. I won't bother to describe this immense being because I truly do not want to remember it any more than necessary. Very simply, this entity looked nothing like anything your finest imagination might conjure up.

Another journey was unfolding. We were moving at a brisk pace. I felt a sensation akin to seasickness. When we stopped, I nearly lost my balance.

I had been taken to a pyramid-like structure lined with mirrors. The colors emanating from these mirrors were so spellbinding that my brain unexpectedly turned into mush.

Sensing my dilemma, Tara placed her hand gently on the small of my back. Then, with a glance to the other being, Tara proceeded to place a long appendage, resembling a finger, to my third eye. I immediately found myself in the lushest of gardens, with long-flowing grass, and trees and flowers in the greatest of abundance. I was in peace.

I was later told that this is how her species handles any overwhelming situation. They simply go to the most beautiful place within their memory sensors.

New Sensations

After what seemed like hours, which probably lasted but a few seconds, I was returned to the pyramid of light particles, and the download of information continued. Unfortunately, my brain quickly reached a point of feeling completely overloaded again. This time, I knew I could no longer handle the level of thoughts that were being transmitted. So I called for Kirael.

As always, Kirael's presence was with me instantaneously, and he proceeded to translate Tara's transmissions into language that I could understand.

Kirael Speaks:

Her name is as you heard it. She is known as Tara and is one of the descendants of the Guardian of Peace and Tranquility. They are known as Ascension-Orientated Light-Charged Particles. Tara's mission is to be of service to any species regaining the knowingness of love.

These particles, such as Tara, are enlightened through pineal gland incarnation and are found amongst matrix energy patterns scattered throughout many universes. It is their task to awaken all that they come in contact with. However, not all react in a positive manner because of the vast vibrational sequencing of their processing codes.

Planets of any awareness level are subject to Tara's light. Incarnate dimensional forces never intercede nor limit her in the awakening she brings forth to ascension forces. In fact, Tara was the guiding force that brought the Intergalactic Frontier Federation (IGFF) to the table. It was also she who brought focus to the abductions of processing units from the many planetary systems.

Through her guidance, the IGFF, a council of twelve representatives, enlightened the federation group charged with the Earth-Lunar system. Through the council's efforts, each system presently vibrates at the level most common to its inhabitants.

The last time Tara interceded fully in this planetary system was at the dawning of the Buddha Light. From there, it was passed onto the masters of multiple awareness. In truth, much of Eastern philosophy integrates her teachings.

Tara was not present on the Earth plane at the time of Jesus. However, it is widely known that she introduced an aspect of her light into Mother Mary when Jesus was still in her womb. This light that was placed within Jesus' pineal gland is called the Ascension Matrix Energy Particle.

Her interactions with any species signify that they are at a stage of evolution to understand the true and full meaning of conceptual love.

When I had the honor of guiding Tara's Light, it was at a time when the decision to re-populate your planet was still in question. It was not clear whether the Third Dimension could be designed to allow a species to evolve to the Fourth Dimension while remaining embodied. In earlier situations, planets similar to Earth were completely eradicated of physical existence at certain stages prior to a planetary shift. This allowed the new life forms a clear awareness to begin new levels of evolution.

Tara explains how those in her council had become aware of multiple societies that had become adept at shift changes. The council had learned that when these societies felt a shift in process, they would retreat underground for survival. It became a new way for developing societies to evolve. The process would be best described as a "reverse mirror reflection of the ego system." This meant that the entity was no longer in the evolutionary process, much like a human in a coma. In this manner, the higher self reduced its conscious alignment or connection with the human to only one strand, through the umbilical cord.

When the Guardian councils of this planetary system viewed this process, they saw that the Earth plane was ready to enter into the next Shift, this time with its population intact.

You might recall that until years ago, the human population was not fully prepared for this new evolutionary experience, even with the presence of Jesus on the Earth plane.

Understand that your third-dimensional matrix is based on possibilities, most of which are yet to be experienced. To that extent, every focus is a possibility. In the last two thousand years, the human life force has proven its resilience and desire to experience a planetary shift. Each member of the human species has evolved into a fully operating system of complex "e-motion energizers." This means that each is now capable of raising the body frequency to align to the Fourth Light vibration.

In preparation for the Shift, the Earth beings' higher selves have been tuning these e-motion energizers, also called matrix crystals. These crystals are found in the cellular matrix within the subcutaneous walls of the physical body. Tuning these matrix crystals regulates the pulsation of each DNA strand. In turn, each strand directs charges to its equivalent non-physical or etheric strand. When this takes place, each strand receives the instruction to begin its journey of incarnation at a higher vibration. This process is also defined as the "prescribed formula for double-stranded DNA to sustain life in a duality-functioning illusion."

This is why your scientists are now detecting the existence of these new strands. Individuals with extended DNA are still the exception. Many lightworkers, however, are feeling this enhancement and are now experiencing the move to the next level, the Fourth Dimension.

Journey into the Fourth Dimension

In her light being presence, Tara shares a vision of how Mother Earth is tentatively foreseeing its inaugural unfolding into the new energy. She shows the lightworkers releasing the confines of duality as they align to a trinity motion of cellular awakening.

In the actual Shift process, Tara sees lightworkers in the process of awakening from their deep sleep during the "three days of darkness." She also sees that the world will appear unsuitable for human life if viewed through the physical eyes. People will have difficulty standing upright because gravity has been altered.

Each cell in the human system will have expanded its matrix energy. Its density will have diminished by 30%. This will create a situation of imbalance which can be brought into alignment only through thought. Your awakening into a fourth-dimensional vibration will require a comprehensive realignment of the way everything is experienced.

To illustrate this, Tara offers a scenario of what will take place when a human sneezes in the Fourth Light energy. The first time you sneeze in this new energy, the sneeze will send you reeling across the room. This is because your body will no longer be functioning on oxygen. By third-dimensional habit, you will have inhaled a large breath prior to this action and then expelled it in a grand push. The difference is that along with your deep breath, you will also have inhaled an extremely large amount of prana into your system. This is because oxygen will be combined with prana in the Fourth Dimension to physically lighten the body system. Then before you know it, the urge to expel all this energy will overtake you, while the gravitational resistance you are accustomed to will be nonexistent. So across the room you go.

Tara wishes for all to get a flavor of this new dimension. In truth, however, there really is nothing that can be shared to prepare the human fully for all the changes to come. Yet, to further assist the masses in better preparing for the awakening into the new light, Tara and I will collaborate to bring forth a work readable by all.

As a sneak preview, our readers will discover that a thought is defined as "a sequencing of reality in formational spontaneity" in the Fourth Dimension. In this energy, they will learn that questioning any segment of the aligned patterns of the thought formation will automatically create a possible holographic solution to experiment with. All potential outcomes will be layered by the manner in which one chooses to experience the end results. Thus, in the Fourth Dimension, no journey will be left to chance.

The Shifting Ego

Yes, the ego will still exist in the Fourth Dimension. However, it will take on a different role. Instead of acting as a shroud surrounding life itself, the ego will be able to adjust to particular individual lessons within a controlled reality. It will be completely controlled by thought. You will raise or lower the density of the ego at will. For example, if you wished to go through a different level of an experience, you could amplify the ego system for a longer duration of time, if that was necessary.

Adjusting the ego system should be practiced fully before the Shift takes place. Even in the density of the Third Dimension, the ego can be adjusted through your cellular awareness. When you accept that the ego is one of your greatest allies and not some sort of troublemaker, you will begin to use it in an advantageous way.

Why is there an ego system? You need only recall the journey of Eve. It was she who saw how detrimental it would be to the human journey to experience the All That Is. Hence, the Creator allowed for the ego system to serve as a veil, so that humankind could experience the Earth plane fully.

Were it not for the veil of your ego, you would have complete control of your thoughts. You would be experiencing everything through the six senses. Everything would be seen in its true nature, and you would want to leave this level of evolution. For this reason, the Creator allowed for an ego system.

How Will We Know?

How will you know that a Great Shift is about to take place? Always before a Great Shift takes place, the planet involved in the shifting process is realigned. The inhabitants of the planet notice things they never saw before. Their physical world is more intricate. The green of the foliage is much brighter and the fragrance of flowers is more delicate.

The five senses are heightened to their fullest potential.

As stated previously, another sign of an impending planetary shift is when energy patterns, such as Tara, align with a planetary focus. When this occurs, it must be acknowledged that the time nears. I, therefore, want to thank Tara for sharing her light with the human world. Love will prevail on Earth, especially now, knowing that Tara's energy is present.

The Almon Report

Only a short time ago, Tara sent her emissary, Almon, to this planet to study the conditions of Earth. His mission was to assess Earth's readiness to accept the ET world into the human reality. Almon's findings were positive for the most part. Yet, he did see that there was a problem with listening amongst the Earth beings. That is, humans hear what they want to hear and seldom focus on what is actually being said.

The Almon Report was used by Tara's council to determine the level of love attained by the collective consciousness of planet Earth. The grade he gave was extremely passable, based on the positive experiences he had in his encounters with humans.

It is with the highest respect that your galactic brothers and sisters prepare to assist the lightworkers in aligning the grid system of Mother Earth. They hold the highest interests of the human world in their hearts. At one time or another, they have experienced similar lesson plans. They know how wonderful it will be for those who choose to make the Shift.

Let the unity begin.

Questions and Answers

Q: How is it that an energy pattern such as Tara, who is herself a direct descendent of a Guardian of Developmental Societies, would refer to Kirael as "Master"?

Kirael: Once you have studied with ones of that esteem, you always want to offer the honor and respect that is their due. You simply know that "Master" is a term held for those who stringently expose Truth.

So those of my light, meaning those who have reached the level where others choose to call us Masters, know that all is in perfection when all is in a constant state of enlightenment. No matter what level of awareness one attains, one never ceases striving to experience the next possibility. One knows that each level of awareness exists only to open new frontiers of ascending potentials.

Q: In all of Mother Earth's history, what has been one of the strangest incarnations of this planet?

Kirael: One of the strangest incarnations on Earth was a composite of machine parts and thought processes. They were sent to mine the gold ore that was found on planet Earth. They erroneously believed that the gold ore was the same as the golden light particles that are the building blocks of a vast array of embodiment processes.

These humanoid entities succeeded in amassing large quantities of this new substance with gold properties. They felt the need to protect it. These entities eventually developed a form of ego and began to compete with each other.

With time, other realms of awareness forgot about the humanoids on planet Earth. They were not considered to be of a valued evolutionary process. Therefore, they had the freedom to experience on a multitude of different levels. They became so advanced in the art of territorial segmentation that a new form of society began to emerge. However, they diminished over time because they were not activated or regenerated in light particles. In other words, they had no soul energy or any way of understanding love.

With many of these early populations of Earth, the intervention of higher powers became imminent. The true essence of the Creator is Love, and it must be present to support any form of evolution. When love is nonexistent, life in any form fails.

Q: How does cloning affect the development of societies?

Kirael: Many of the societies that were entrenched in the duality consciousness began their "de-evolution" by replicating themselves. Called cloning today, in the past it was defined as "exact duplication of consciously aware particles."

What must be understood is that while the cellular body can be replicated in perfection, there remains only one soul, or higher self, for all its aspects. The danger is when the higher self has to control two aspects of one incarnation (the originator self and the clone), it must split its consciousness. That is, each aspect must operate in diminished capacity. Lesson plans, therefore, become entangled because the originator self is still striving to evolve, while the clone has little energy to do the same. With a diminished awareness of its higher self, the clone has little desire to learn or "do the journey." Then each is left with limited connection to the source of its origination, Creator God.

When the inhabitants of a planet implement the process of cloning, it is only a matter of time before the cloned entities become abominable. The galactic group, known as the "Grays," is an example of one such situation. These particular ET's were the last survivors of a cloned society. They had escaped the collapse of their systems just before their own doing annihilated it.

Before the actual collapse of these worlds, drone ships are usually sent in search of both new arenas and/or ways to reproduce their life forms. They travel through space searching for inhabitable planetary systems where little resistance might be met. Their first choice is a planet where the entire society has been eradicated due to the misuse of their abundance. Their second choice is a planet whose society is so intent on self-indulgence that they are obsessed with protecting their personal wealth. On such a planet, they know that the inhabitants are so self-centered that they pay little attention to things not directly affecting their private worlds.

Needless to say, the latter condition is what the Grays found on the Earth plane. Initially, the Grays were successful in abducting humans onto their advance craft. However, the high vibration of the soul consciousness of this planet prevailed. The invasion attempts of these renegade forces into the Earth plane were thwarted. In truth, many more humans would have surrendered willingly and boarded the advance craft had it not been for the higher light of the One Consciousness that was aware of the drama unfolding. Thus, further attempts at human abductions by the Grays were aborted.

Even clones must respond to the councils of higher awareness. By losing their connection with the Creator, these cloned entities jeopardized the relations of interstellar travelers and set back inter-galactic alliances many, many years.

Q: There are those who believe that humans are closely connected to the worlds of dolphins and whales. Would you comment on that, please?

Kirael: I often speak of these beings as your elder brothers and sisters because, like humans, whales and dolphins are known to shed salt tears.

At a given point in their evolution, whales and dolphins learned to live both in and out of the water. Their legacy for humans is the grid system of magnetic energy patterns that surrounds the Earth both in and out of the water. It is a legacy because the whales and dolphins have made this information accessible to humans in the etheric records. To this day, whales and dolphins still navigate around the world using these gridlines.

In the early stages of this incarnation, humans utilized their sixth sense for traveling, much like the dolphins and whales. Most likely, the dolphins were the ones that taught ancient explorers how to use this vibrational grid system to navigate by.

Current day humans use approximately 10% of their brain to function whereas dolphins, as well as whales, use 100%. Only when dolphins sleep do they shut down approximately 50% of their massive thought systems. The other 50% directs energy to parts of its anatomy to rejuvenate. In the new matrix after the Shift, humans will regenerate body vibrations in a similar manner.

The whales, the record keepers of all time, are currently working with other systems of life to prepare for the Shift. They are coordinating the atmospheric conditions that humans will need for operating their light bodies in the Fourth Dimension. Without the information that the whales hold of Mother Earth, the Shift will not take place. Thus, given the vital role that whales play in the Shift, it makes sense to become more active in their protection. It is true that the whales themselves could make greater attempts to protect themselves. However, Creator law allows whales, like humans, to have free will to choose their own destiny.

Q: It is known that repopulating the planet was, at one time, in question. What was the turning point that persuaded the powers of light to go forth?

Kirael: The time referred to is when planet Earth had sunken into a period where only the dark presence permeated the inhabitable land. Societies had plummeted, for the people believed that the Creator no longer watched over their evolutionary energy. They felt that they had been left alone to create their own levels of awareness. This took place in the period between the Lemurian and Atlantean civilizations.

Many spiritual seekers of that time believed that the only way to survive the great upheaval was to disconnect their energy in any manner they could, so they gave up and denounced love. Those who had already attained the level of lightworkers were sent from the sinking continent of Lemuria to Atlantis through the process of molecular transportation. All who remained in between were left to feel that the world had come to an end. In this feeling of hopelessness, they felt nothing could save them. So they allowed the forces of the dim world to permeate their existence.

This led to a debate amongst the councils questioning whether to allow such a state of dimmed force to continue. After all, it was argued that there were many planetary systems capable of hosting entities of dimmed realities.

In the end, it was those of the Guidance Realm who held the one thing that really mattered, hope. They made it known that if it were the pronouncement of the council to continue life, they, the Guidance Realm, would stand ready to assist the world of humans for all time to come.

What a commitment that turned out to be!

9

Completion: Religion, Spirituality, and the Great Shift

Kirael's Numerology:
A "9" day indicates that completion is at hand, and it is a time to move on. Recognize that you have the choice to complete anything on this day. The beauty of a completion day is that it always leads to a new beginning with number one again.

Author's Insights:

U ntil now, there has been an inexhaustible span of illusionary time available for repeating life lessons over and over again. The number of third-dimensional lives that were possible has seemed endless. However, time is no longer on your side. You are entering the phase of completion which leads to the Shift.

After the Shift, many old lesson plans, such as chronic physical ailments or deep anger and harsh judgments, will no longer be available to be played out as life experiences. This is why so many are working diligently on these lessons in this lifetime. But before you come down hard on yourself for having a chronic disease, or for holding onto emotional scars from the past and feeling as if you are just not "getting it," realize that the Creator has allowed for even the minutest details to be fully graced.

This requires faith. In fact, your ability to hold the line of faith is in direct proportion to your evolutionary growth.

So take a new step in faith. Complete old lesson plans that have held you back for so long, and enter into new and wondrous beginnings. In the final chapter of this work, again, let truth be your guide.

Kirael Speaks:

Up to this point, the primary focus of this work has been that this Earth is a matrix of space and time. That the Earth is the expression of the wise intentions of the All That Is. That humans are encouraged to play out every imaginable potentiality through the five-sensory experience. That each has the right to a full measure of life awareness, no matter how bold or intricate. That the Creator brought Its energy to a level of such intensity on the Earth plane to allow imagined separation of Itself while creating journeys to fill its every sense. And that the learning just continues to expand with no end in sight, for the end merely means moving to the next level of awakening.

Allow me to pose a number of questions from which to further the truths of this work. What if humans were to hold truth that there is only one pattern of light that is the source of all life force? Or what if the collective energy was not about one body of beliefs being right and the other wrong? More importantly, what if the entire collective consciousness of spirit-based understandings were based on interpretation and that was the only difference that existed? Yes, we have already asked these questions, and they need to be asked yet again to create a space where humanity can unite in love and healing.

Specifically, let us pursue the premise that religion and spiritualism are one and the same, and only the interpretation is different. I begin by defining the words "religionist" and "spiritualist" to see how the words themselves create a sense of separation.

Religionist

A religionist is one who is a follower of a prescribed set of doctrines or dogma with very little questioning of such doctrines. Religionists rely on the cumulative perception of the author, or authors, who are attempting to create new precepts, based on an existing set of speculations.

We have already seen in an earlier chapter that most religious texts available to us today were handed down in ancient times through song or storytelling. The Bible and other religious texts became more condensed over eons of time through oral traditions. Thus, the margin for interpretation was ever present. At a given point, the oral traditions were put into written form. Some writings of great significance to the world were intentionally not included in the final single-text process of the Bible. Would not a truth-seeking person want to know of these things?

The world of the religionist is based on the writings of the Bible. The Creator is viewed as an all-powerful being which rules over human awareness. It watches over every move of every human, so as to judge the worthiness of soul. It appoints a select few to speak for this all-powerful being, thereby leaving those to determine that which is deemed right or wrong. Hence, judgment prevails amongst man, and one man must follow another human's interpretations of right or wrong in order to enter the so-called Promised Land. Fear and guilt are all too often what separates them from their Creator.

Indeed, one religion holds it truth that one man is appointed by his human peers to a supreme position akin to God. He alone is the one human with the right to communicate directly with the all-powerful essence known as God. This same human representative of the Creator also forgives the sins of those who show the correct amount of repentance, or metes out punishment to those who do not.

The ideas here are not meant to criticize any given dogma. Instead, it is to show that the established belief systems have discouraged people from questioning the written word. After all, if a crack were found in a dam that held the great waters, the danger would be of the crack becoming larger. Eventually, the crack would become a split in the foundation, and the waters would burst forth in a flood. Likewise, a crack in established belief systems would open up a flood of new questions. Recorded history would come tumbling out for all to see anew.

Perhaps it is time to let the waters flow: to let our hearts guide the outcome of this awesome journey called life.

Spiritualist

A spiritualist is one who believes that societies are in constant states of awakening. Spiritualists recognize the evolution of change. They seek greater clarity of the various possibilities that each new opportunity brings into their reality. They understand that all parts of their life lesson plans must be thoroughly experienced in order to complete each lesson fully. They do not allow the belief systems of others to dissuade them from the potentiality of their own evolutionary journeys.

It is the reality of the spiritualists to sift through the many possibilities until they feel that truth has brought them to their own knowingness. Only then does it become clear that they need not adhere to any established belief for its own sake. Rather, they can move immediately into new ways of understanding the next part of their evolutionary journeys.

For the spiritualist, the evolutionary journey is a cumulative experience wherein love is the resilient force. Each vibrational presence has the right to heal back into love.

The spiritualist considers any holy text, including the Bible, a map to help them understand those who came before them. Such writings remind the spiritualist of a time when humans regarded each other as brothers and sisters. The spiritualist discovers how different interpretations of such texts can lead to new outcomes. When carefully read, each period of the matrix in holy texts reveals words used to maintain order of the people in those times. The spiritualist sees how the original "Consciousness of One" was quickly redirected into systems of control, and created for the self-preservation of a few.

In the world of the spiritualist, the Creator is recognized as the Omnipresence of all Light in Creation and each human as a particle of this Light. Hence, in simple terms, the religionist believes in the Spirit of One, whereas the spiritualist believes in the Oneness of Spirit.

Going Beyond

There is no longer any reason for religionists and spiritualists to be criticized for their beliefs. Each of you has brought your light to the Earth plane to be a part of an evolutionary transformation of the planet. Each of you has a lesson plan which involves questioning belief systems handed down from the past as part of your journey. The truths you seek are not readily found in the written word or in the words of any one person. The answers you seek begin with the process of questioning in your heart the truths of others.

My friends, when you begin to question what you have been told, you begin to align with your spirituality.

The truth for each is what resonates in the heart. To feel that one has to persuade another only shows that the one doing the persuading is the one least convinced of his or her own journey.

Simply seek your own truth. Light your light so bright that others who seek to evolve their consciousness will, in turn, begin to seek their own truths.

The Shift will begin inwardly. The search outside oneself will be for those who need to journey in the third-dimensional Earth matrix.

The Matrix of Thought

When Creation, another name for the Creator, began the journey of thought, it literally exploded into various degrees of potential. Each thought amassed into a collection of energy patterns aligned to the central order. Each had in its own value stream a multiple response system that could be transferred from one level to another. These levels were dimensional standards in which repetitive conglomerates of unified particle vibrations actually clung together.

The system became the advancement of thought. Values needed to be assigned for the sake of synchronicity. What developed was a numerical system that could hold within its vibration a collective consciousness. The energies of the numbers then proceeded to employ their own growth by assigning particle lines measurable in increments.

These numbers created a systematic level of awareness that held the vibrations to certain levels. This, in itself, was the assignment of dimensional separators. Dimensional separators could define the world of thought into experiences. Interactions between source and maintainable linear thought projections could be known.

At this point, the real excitement began. Here, the Creator could align Its experiential thoughts and allow the journey of Its own evolution to exist on multiple levels, or dimensions. Within these dimensions, numerous vibrational journeys could amass in collective energy.

In its origination, the system of numbers was a simple way of determining the equitable foundation assigned by the Creator. Numbers held the truths of the ages. By prescribing to each number an auditory vibration infused with light particles, the possibility arose that all which seemed chaotic at first was in fact unified in a system of numbers called a matrix. Together, it became a system of sound and light by integrating all possibilities into an observable journey played out as sequentially malleable vibrations taking on the illusion of mass. This illusionary mass would serve as the conservatory of all self-aware aspects of creation.

For now, just allow the resonance of these words to play within your system.

Why This Matrix?

The Earth matrix is one of the few remaining planetary vibrations that still operates through the five-sensory experience.

The representative aspects on Earth have been spiraling in their lessons for millenia of time. Each life has followed a sequence of lessons, until no lessons remain unlearned.

Over the last two thousand years, humanity in its entirety has moved into a collective agreement with Creation to escalate the lesson plan. Indeed, many of the lessons being played out today are those that have not been fully recognized. Hence, the universal e-motion of the Earth matrix has opened en masse in the light of collective self-empowerment to design these final stages of the Third Dimension.

For instance, a person abused as a child generally abuses others. In most cases, it takes multiple lifetimes to work through the many potential lessons inherent in such experiences. This has been part of the growth system over the last two thousand years. But for many, the process of learning has evolved into spirals of over-reaction. Attempts to learn all possible lessons have reached a point referred to as the "overcure."

This must now come to closure. It is no longer possible to continue growing through multiple lifetimes. Thus, a new stage has been implemented to break these unending cycles of overcure. Many have come onto the Earth plane as "cycle breakers" for those bogged down in spirals of overcure. Cycle breakers are incarnate now to bring the long sought-after cures to the ills of this matrix reality.

The job of cycle breakers is far more difficult than any other lesson plan they may have chosen. First, as cycle breakers, they must experience the illness or dis-ease firsthand. Then, they must experience the illness to whatever level necessary to engage their higher selves. Finally, their job is to align other patterns of life forces within their spiritual influence to create the collective awareness that brings forth the cures.

This is possible because the collective consciousness has awakened far more than ever before. The unity of soul families has ascended to a new level, and collective efforts have risen to a new crescendo. Thus, no longer is the energy known as Mother Earth willing to be patient. She now needs completion so that she, along with her inhabitants, can move to the next matrix of evolution, the Fourth Dimension.

Until now, the matrix has vibrated in a constant hum of sound and light so that each lesson could be played out at its own separate pace. Now, everything is being geared to shift simultaneously, and all the players of this illusion are embracing completion collectively. Many may feel isolated, although they are in fact part of the whole. Many may have no awareness of the Shift and continue in patterns of overcure, yet they are being drawn into a need for completion in parts of their lives.

There are many cycle breakers on the planet now. You know who you are.

Lightworkers Amassing

Who are these cycle breakers, really?

They are those that pray and meditate; they are those who choose to seek their answers from the spiritual forces that exist beyond the matrix energies. They listen and interact with their higher selves. They believe that love is the only answer to the human existence. And collectively, they are amassing in an awareness known as the lightworkers.

The world is moving into a state of consciousness that is unstoppable at this point. Everything is being stretched to a new vibration. Lightworkers are the ones shifting out of the energies of the third-dimensional matrix. They do not need to take stands on issues at the exclusion of others. Lightworkers have the ability to choose from within their hearts on any subject matter. They know that it is for each to know in his or her heart what truth is.

Cycle breakers are lightworkers. They are one and the same, for collectively, they know that love is the only answer to existence.

The Genesis Matrix Revisited

You will recall that eons of space and time ago, light particles watched as the Creator brought together the smallest particles of light from which was emitted a sound. This sound amassed a force of golden particles so brilliant that they shone as clear crystal. These brilliant crystals began to form their own vibration, and the core of Mother Earth was born.

Within the crystal core of Mother Earth resided the resonance of love, her heartbeat. The plan was for this pulsating sound to remain constant, deep within Mother Earth's core. The tone and vibration of her core would remain there as long as there were humans who needed to experience a matrix of duality. It would resonate the sound of love detectable by any who chose to hear it.

Also registered in her crystal core was that Mother Earth's heartbeat would signify the time for evolution when the mass consciousness was ready to move beyond the bounds of duality. This would signify that Earth would evolve its energy to the next level in love. And in love, her inhabitants would move to the next level as well.

The Shift you are now experiencing was designed to take place when Jesus walked the Earth. However, it became clear that human evolution was not then at a level commensurate to the Shift energies. Thus, it became necessary to revise the plan.

A new journey was opened. This is the journey that all are on today, the journey of completion. The matrix in its current energies must evolve. The heartbeat of Mother Earth has registered this change in human evolution, and she must now move to the next level. This assures all humankind a place to experience the Fourth Dimension.

Beginning or End: Your Choice

For all that exists, there is a defined purpose. More specifically, for all who have reached this stage of Earth's history, there is a reason for being incarnate on the Earth plane now. Each person reading this work is experiencing the evolutionary act of being human. This can only be accomplished by knowing the heart essence of evolutionary progression.

The complex expression of your higher self, the part of you called human, has searched many millennia to finally reach a space where a planet and its inhabitants can simultaneously raise the vibration of all life. You have chosen to assist Mother Earth by utilizing the force of love. In that, you have made the conscious decision to be here for the process. Take to heart, my friends, that by having chosen to be a part of this awesome experience, you shall be honored for all illusionary time to come.

Will it be easy? Can the light of the soul, harnessed in a human body, prevail? That depends on the mass consciousness of lightworkers discovering truth in love. It also depends on the level of trust found within this love. The final element is for the lightworkers to amass enough passion in love to complete their human journeys.

And the journey once again leads back to the beginning: to the trinity of Truth, Trust, and Passion.

Questions and Answers

Q: The trinity of God the Father, the Son, and the Holy Spirit is often projected as separate beings. How do you in the Guidance Reality view this trinity?

Kirael: As opposed to being one, many do see the Father, Son, and Holy Spirit as separate. While they are a complex systematic vibration of the whole, it is possible to identify them separately, as long as all understand their true unity within a trinity formation.

The Father/Creator is defined as the All-Light Presence or as the All-Existence, which is embodied in Light and constant in Love.

The Son/Christ is the All-Thought Consciousness of Creation through which all must pass to become enlightened, or even better, "in-lightened." The Son/Christ is that part of the Creator which is aligned with the physical world. It is the part that evolved into a light being while still on this plane.

The Holy Spirit/Ghost is all that has been released in the form of Creator Light to experience the feeling of separation in evolution. This energy is in alliance with the mass consciousness of all evolving energies that allows you to be you, me to be me, and all to be one. Thus, the Holy Spirit/Ghost is the force of energy in formation.

Q: Is the ego a matrix?

Kirael: Remember that the ego is a thought pattern. The ego is itself a matrix of conscious awareness used to filter the knowing of the higher self into human experience. Mother Earth has a defined ego as does a human. It is a collective magnetic energy grid that allows her to resonate with the evolution of her inhabitants. As mass awareness increases, the magnetic energy grid surrounding Mother Earth lessens in force. This allows the shift of the planet and her inhabitants to move simultaneously into full vibration.

The density that exists within current incarnations must be nullified, and a less dense vibration must be set to function on all levels of this new vibration. This will influence not only the human ego system, but will also reset the influence of the collective ego matrix that defines Earth's position within the universe.

In the Fourth Dimension, the human ego needs to be reduced in density by as much as 75%. This will depend greatly on which level of awareness you vibrate to in the Fourth Dimension. As with your brethren of the neighboring worlds, you will have access to thought screens that will display collective consciousness on varying levels of ego-sorted realities. They will range from full density to pure light formations, and each will have the choice of how to proceed. In the higher levels of awareness, you will be able to raise or lower your ego awareness through instantaneous thought manifestation.

In its basic form, the ego will be a screening mechanism used to bring forth lesson plans that can be worked on in two or more levels at the same time. Your ego will assist you so that you will no longer have to go through the long, drawn-out lesson plans, and you will be able to see the truth of your four-body healing at once. Not only will you be able to see them, you will be able to deal with them one at a time or collectively through multiple-functioning brain waves.

Q: Lightworkers are often part of grassroots organizations. What is your definition of "grassroots"?

Kirael: What is grassroots? I would liken it to what takes place when grass is mowed. When a lawnmower makes its first swath in a field of grass, each blade that is cut sends out a signal to all the remaining blades of grass about what is taking place. Each root immediately begins to interact with the next root until the entire lawn is collectively activated to begin a phase of new growth.

Grassroots means that no entity in and of itself is held responsible for doing all the work, nor for that matter, for receiving all the credit when a mission is completed. All share as co-creators in the collective endeavor.

Q: How close are we to the Shift?

Kirael: When you come to the clarity that the beauty in your life is on levels never seen before, and all five senses are at heightened sensitivities never imagined before, you realize just how close to the full Shift you are.

Many, many, many of you have already begun to experience the beauty of the Shift, some of you kicking and screaming in the process. Yet each journey that a person experiences at this level of awareness is meant to initiate the awakening into new states of evolution. Each begins to experience through the sixth sense. Each senses the intervention of spirit in this reality.

As a particle of the God Creator, you said at one time, "Please, let me be a part of this Shift." And the Creator said, "You know there are some major tests that will be experienced during this time. If you go down to Earth and act like a 'human,' you are going to be tested like one. The test will be this, my little particle friend, to remember that you are a particle of the God Light in the human form."

You, the lightworker, are the hope of Creation. If you hold steadfast in the light of Creation, you will begin to heal the world. Healing begins one heart at a time, and that is only the beginning. There are those of you who are destined to create a space for the multitudes to heal and see that there is great hope on the horizon.

The Shift is here, my friends, and you can't turn back. You've made a commitment to be the Creator's Light incarnate. So if your life is a bit disheveled, take a breath. Here is my challenge to you, the lightworker: Recognize your own love and beauty. Don't get caught in the chaos. Search your heart for love each and every moment. Decide what you want to do, and step forward again. Don't get nervous. Just do the journey.

From the beginning of the illusion of time, there has been but one simple focus—for the Creator to experience the feeling of separation from Its own vibration. You might ask: But why? If the Creator is the All That Is, why would It want to experience this illusion?

The answer is, because It could.

The Matrix System of Numbers:
Guiding Your Life with Kirael's Numerology

The planet Earth is a construct of a matrix based almost entirely on numbers. The other two factors in this equation are sounds and lights, which are emitted by numbers in varying combinations.

Numbers have played an unending role in the development of all evolutionary systems. There are no absolutes, for there are limitless numerical combinations. When one is bound by an absolute, the possibility for growth is nullified.

Your life is based on an entire matrix of numerical systems. It moves in endless patterns of lights and pulsations created from the numbers of the matrix. Your life, like the life of the planet, has the possibility for limitless evolutionary growth. This is why an awareness of numerology can be important for in your life.

For thousands of years, people have understood how the stars influence their lives, perhaps not recognizing that astrology is based on numerical equations. Now, you may see the beauty of how numerology affects your life on a daily basis.

Here is how numerology works with the date of November 25 or 11/25, for example. Take all the numbers of the month and the day, and add them separately: 1+1+2+5=9. The single numerical digit that remains is a nine, which represents *completion*. So on this "9" day, try to bring to closure as much unfinished business and unresolved issues in your life as possible, for it leads to new beginnings.

By using Kirael's numerology every day, you will find how a simple understanding of the energy of numbers can guide you to make new choices in your life. Your life will evolve in harmony with the universe.

1 God-Creator

A "1" day is your opportunity to reconnect to the God Light within you and to know that something completely new is about to begin. It is interesting that this day always follows a completion day.

2 Duality

A "2" day reminds you to be aware that yin/yang situations are all around you. On this day, it is best to take a look at where your life is, and to move your thoughts into a higher trinity level of understanding.

3 Trinity

On a "3" day, be guided by the trinity of Truth, Trust, and Passion. Feel it create a new essence of love awakening about you. Something bright and beautiful is about to take place in your life.

4 Thought

On a "4" day, be very conscious of your thinking processes. Keep your thoughts extremely positive, because in the world of thought, they can readily be manifested in any direction.

5 Love

On a "5" day, watch for anything around you that can resonate in love and take advantage of if. Be in love on a "5" day and feel love surrounding you. When you choose love as the foundation of each decision, all comes to perfection in light.

6 *Mastery*

A "6" day reminds you that you are in control of your life. Leave nothing undone. Complete all lessons. As master of your own life, it is your great day to make masterful decisions and to ascend to new levels of conscious awareness.

7 *Transition*

A "7" day signals that it is time to move on. A day of great awareness, you can experience the day on multiple levels simultaneously and move from one level to the next. You are in the flow of change and transformation.

8 *Infinity*

An "8" day signifies that the present is being shared in two realities at the same time, as in a loop. You are in simultaneous connection with both spirit and matrix energies. If you can remain in the center of the loop looking out at both directions, you are in a good space.

9 *Completion*

A "9" day indicates that completion is at hand, and it is a time to move on. Recognize that you have the choice to complete anything on this day. The beauty of a completion day is that it always leads to a new beginning with number one again.

Acknowledgements

My warmest aloha and appreciation go out to the thousands of people that were led to the first work *Kirael: The Great Shift*. With the support—especially the feedback that we received from you, the reader—there was reason to write this new work.

I would like to extend my light onto the Kirael energy. His love and patience on this project clearly inspired this team of dedicated lightworkers to bring forth the enchantment you will experience in this work.

The team:

A heartfelt thank you to Reverend Carol Morishige for her commitment to see this project through from its conception to the final printing. With her love shining on this work, I know in my heart that you will feel the light of Kirael. Her vibration has so melded with the Kirael light that she has maintained the integrity that is seen on every page.

Where would I have been without the patience and enthusiasm of Lori Domingo? An English instructor by profession, she needed to take the sentence structures of a seventh-dimensional being and convert them to proper English while not losing the flavor of this divine information. Can you imagine working in those two worlds simultaneously?

Karen Yue inspired the editing team to constantly refine the work, making it more clearly readable for the readers. Her continual need for clarification was a blessing not only for the reader, but also for myself.

Lauren, our editor consultant, was extremely generous with her time and energy. Her consistent attention to the details allowed for all to "sharpen their hooks."

Lance Agena impassioned the work with the golden particles that flow throughout the work. His blinding speed in completing the layouts was critical in bringing forth the work to the world.

Tom Holowach showed his strength for accuracy, a key to maintaining the structured force of the matrix. Thanks for engineering this vibration to a point where the readers can see the next level.

Melvin Morishige was dedicated in focusing on the production and operation of the overall project. His willingness to go the extra mile was invaluable.

My gratitude also to the transcribers: Karen Boyle, Sherri-Anne Kamaka, Susan Kiyosaki, Sonja Langley, Barbara Miyashiro, Karen Nielsen, Lisa Ann Quison, Marni Suu Ellgren, and Fay Shimoko

Special thanks to my wife, Patti. As you have awakened yourself to heal, many of us around you have chosen the same path. If willingness to complete the journey is the test of life, I know you have already passed.

Finally, no words could ever sufficiently express my gratitude to the staff, church council and special project volunteers of the Honolulu Church of Light, who have shared their love and support: Kehau Agena, Dave Bower, Sue Bowman, Lynn Braekevelt, Karen Eakman, Jerry Fujioka, Diana George, Gail Jan Kaneshiro, Paul Kaneshiro, Phillip Lau, Stacie Lau, George Lopez, Ron Maestro, Donn Marutani, Rev. Akihiro and Valerie Moriwaki, Carey Norby, Dennis Shipman, Frances Shomura, Silke Vogelmann-Sine Ph.D, Revs. Albert and Thelma Spencer, Jane Starn DrPH, RN, Rick Sterling, James and Rose Taylor, and Christopher Tourtellot.

Last but not least, to the countless lightworkers who have supported our mission of love and healing, we humbly express our thankfulness for your kind words and generosity. Whether our paths fleetingly cross or we, hand in hand, move forward in love, we will forever hold you, our brothers and sisters of Mother Earth in the Creator's Light.

Aloha,

Fred Sterling

About the Author

Reverend Fred Sterling is the Head Pastor and Director of the Honolulu Church of Light. He is first and foremost a man of the heart, a healer, a person of unusual depth and contrast whose consciousness is rooted in the rich soil of life experiences.

At the Honolulu Church of Light, he has emerged as a pioneering healer, author of two books, host of two radio programs and a weekly television program called "The Rev." With all this, he still holds truth that his most important role is that of medium for the wise and loving non-physical energy called Kirael, and through this, has touched the lives of many people around the globe.

Fred Sterling has embraced the adventure of life more passionately than even he thought possible. What validates his work as a Minister, Healer and Author are precisely his life experiences. They have allowed him to cultivate a sense of candidness and authenticity. What you see is what you get; on the street or in a seminar room, his style is fully engaged and extemporaneous.

He lives with his family in Honolulu, Hawaii, and is currently working on his third book, on four-body healing.

Fred Sterling is available for seminars, and for individual or group Kirael sessions.

For more information about the author and his work, visit www.inward.com or contact the Honolulu Church of Light, 1-800-390-1886.

Also by Rev. Fred Sterling

Kirael: The Great Shift

Atlantis, Lemuria, the three days of darkness, ETs, UFOs, soul evolution: these are the backdrop to the most amazing, the most profound evolutionary event in human history—the Great Shift.

With truth, trust and passion, let Kirael skillfully guide you on the most fascinating journey of all time—the love, healing, and triumphant ascension of self and Mother Earth. Just by holding this book, your healing journey begins.

Kirael's insights into the higher realms of love, joy, and fulfillment will heal your feelings of loneliness, confusion, and fear. After all, how could you have come so far if it wasn't time for you to find the answers to the mysteries of life?

"Kirael: The Great Shift *is a fascinating read with valid and important information that is useful for the extraordinary frequency shifts that are occurring! I highly recommend it.*

I look forward to more from Kirael and Rev. Fred Sterling!"

—Jonathan Goldman, author of "Healing Sounds," SHA Director, Sound Healing Pioneer

"Rev. Fred Sterling brings a message of love and caring that removes dark places in the soul and gives hope. He awakens us to the experience that we can live our lives from the knowledge that we are connected to universal wisdom. He brings deep healing to all those who truly want to crate inner peace."

—Silke Vogelmann-Sine, Ph.D, Psychologist, Honolulu, Hawaii

Want more?

Let Kirael be your guide.

The Great Shift is here. Learn more about it with Kirael as your guide. The information is timeless in nature, yet fitting to the events that shape your life as the global shift in conciousness moves into high gear.

You can choose to play an extraordinary part in the awakening of the planet to the Shift or you can choose to endure the events that surround you as best you can. It is your choice.

Choose to be awakened. Join the thousands of lightworkers who already have--then be on the leading edge of the Shift.

For the most current information on the Shift:

- Subscribe to the "Kirael Shift Reports," issued monthly via email* or in printed form.

- Attend "An Evening with Kirael" live channeling sessions, held monthly in the Honolulu Church of Light, Honolulu, Hawaii.

- Listen to the audiotape recordings of "An Evening with Kirael" (when unable to attend the sessions in person).

- Tune in to "The Great Shift with Fred Sterling" weekly Internet/radio broadcast.

- Speak with Fred Sterling and Kirael, and guest lightworkers on the program.

- Obtain your meditation, prayer, and other "tools for the Shift" products. See catalog that follows.

- Be a part of the inward.com family—where lightworkers are amassing in love.

*FREE OF CHARGE with membership to **inward.com**

See catalog on following pages
For more information, call 1-800-390-1886 or
Go to www.inward.com

Inward.com

A home for seekers, dedicated to the truths of love and healing; a place to learn about the global shift in consciousness and how it affects you.

You will find a wealth of information and resources on a wide variety of topics, including:

- Monthly Kirael Shift Reports
- Photon energy forecasts
- On-Line healing room
- Kirael's numerology
- Library of channeled articles
- Tools for the Shift, and much more…

"The Great Shift with Fred Sterling"
Weekly Internet/Radio Broadcast

Connect to the program through inward.com

Listeners have the opportunity to call in and talk live with Fred Sterling and his guests. In the second hour of the program, Rev. Sterling moves his consciousness aside and allows Kirael to bring his loving wisdom through.

Inward.com *is a grassroots, non-profit effort designed and run by volunteers and part-time staff at the Honolulu Church of Light.*

Experience a Live Session with Kirael

Get your copy of these sessions with Kirael, recorded live in Honolulu in digital stereo. $10.00 each.

I.D. # "An Evening with Kirael" 90-minute Audiotapes

72-0001	Unmasking the Stranger in Your Relationships
72-0002	The New Church
72-0003	Warriors of Light
72-0004	The Awakened Dreams of Australia
72-0005	The May 5th Planetary Alignment
72-0007	Galactic Realities
72-0008	Existing Outside the Matrix
72-0009	Living Within the Matrix
72-0010	The Ancient Teachings of Tara: A Galactic Encounter
72-0111	Healing Karma
72-0012	The Origins of Christmas
72-0101	The Galactic Connection
72-0102	Passion: The Fire Within
72-0103	The Great Shift Update: Where Are We Now?

"I would like to express my gratitude for Kirael's books and tapes. By incorporating the guidance and tools, I am able to navigate life's bumps with far more grace and equanimity."

Jalene Greer

Publisher, Auroran Holistic Journal

***To order or for further information
on the annual tape subscription,
Call toll-free 1-800-390-1886,
or email: Shopkirael@yahoo.com***
Order on-line at www.inward.com

Audiotapes by Kirael

Recorded in Digital Stereo $ 9.95 each

Angels

The angelic realities are made up of soul love. They do not sit in judgment of you. They just choose to love you. Each of you has several angels working with you, helping to bring more Light into your life. Learn more of their importance on Earth for the Shift. Item #7201

Aspects, Splinters, Twin Flame Souls

To be in the Third Dimension, you must have made certain agreements to experience all that you desire to experience on the Earth plane. About every seventh year, you experience a shift in consciousness (a splinter) that is the result of a new part of your life plan moving into place. This is all part of the evolution of your soul. Item #7202

Christ Consciousness

Master Jesus came to the Earth plane with a beautiful message of healing through Love. Oftentimes, the message has been veiled. In this tape, Kirael reveals parts of Jesus' life seldom discussed today. Item #7203

Female Energies That Surrounded Christ

In the Bible there is very little mention of the female energies that surrounded Master Jesus. Kirael shares how the female essences such as Mother Mary, Martha, Mary Magdalene and others were in a position to greatly influence the historical events of that time. Item #7204

Sharing Life With Your Ego

The ego is a very beautiful part of your evolution. The ego that you are so quick to judge is not as bad as you might think, for without it there would be no Third Dimension. The whole process is to learn how to heal the ego, go beyond it, because beyond the ego is the God reality. Item #7208

Signature Cell Healing

Signature Cell Healing works with the Creator's essence in the body—the signature cell. This process allows the cellular clarity of the embodiment to awaken on all levels. It goes beyond the five senses and promotes healing in the etheric body—where there is no fear. Item # 7209

Transitioning into the Light

Kirael's gives us insights into the process of completing a lifetime and transitioning into the Light. Keep an open mind as you listen to his profound wisdom and allow your heart to open to a new level of awareness. Item #7211

The Great Shift

Every 2,000 years the Earth plane undergoes a shift in consciousness. Today, we stand at the doorway to the shift into the Fourth Dimension. Big changes are ahead. There is a raising of mass consciousness that will involve healing Mother Earth and the healing of self. Choose to move through the Shift in beauty and grace. Item #7206

Photon Energy

The greatest evolutionary event in history is Mother Earth's entrance into the Photon Energy that will take us into the Fourth Dimension. These events will bring changes that need not cause fear. Find out how the Photon Energy can be used to heighten manifestations through your love. Item #7207

The Galactic Brotherhood

Please do not see them as a threat. See them as peaceful beings of light, for they have chosen to assist humanity through the Shift. The Sirians, Pleiadians, Andromedans, and other galactic societies are here in our atmosphere. Each galactic society has a stake in the outcome of our post-Shift reality. Product #7205

Time Space–The Illusion

Time is an illusion. The space known as the "zone" is defined and measured by the brain. In the brain, there are pulses of energy. Between these pulses is a space where your true consciousness resides. Quantum Physics, New Time Physics, DNA, & more! Item #7210

Call Toll-free 1-800-390-1886
or visit *www.inward.com*

Videotapes

The Shift To Your Higher Self

An easy-to-follow program about the mystic art of healing yourself in body, mind, soul and emotions. Covers Prana Breathing, Masterminding, Prayer, Meditation. Narrated by Rev. Fred Sterling and Rev. Carol Morishige. Produced in a professional TV studio. 60 minutes VHS. **Item #2401 - $19.95**

The Messenger

An exclusive TV interview with Kirael from the Seventh Dimension. Interviewed by Rev. Carol Morishige, Kirael discusses the journey from fear to love and how to embrace the changes with love that the new millennium will bring. Produced in a professional TV studio. 60 minutes VHS. **Item #TP1011-$ 19.95**

Music CDs

Unmask the Stranger

The Band of Light

Through Kirael's guidance and the talented musical gifts of Rev. Akihiro Moriwaki and George Lopez, you can musically follow every chapter of Kirael's book, "Kirael: The Great Shift." **Item #7302 - $15.95**

"Every time you play this CD, Mother Earth receives

a blessing and healing." —Kirael

Peace On Earth

The Band of Light

This newest CD is a magnificent tribute to the greatest desire we all hunger for in our hearts. Every lyric speaks to your soul; every sound voices our yearning for peace. Eleven songs: Peace On Earth, Dear God, We Are The Children, Heart to Heart, Peace Prayer, Rapture, Why, The Message, Don't Lose Your Way, Spread The Word, Believe in Jesus, Angels All Around. **Item #7303 - $15.95**

Healing CDs

New from Kirael!

The Power of Healing Prayers

Features Kirael and background mediation music. Kirael creates nine prayers that guide you to heal and to change your life: Start the Day, Release Fears, Heal the Physical Body, Balance and Center the Emotions, Understand the Children, Release Anger with Love, and Heal from the Loss of a Loved One.

"It's so beautifully put together! I learned how to pray from listening to this CD. You never get tired of listening to these prayers. It's a lifeline for me."—Clara Okazaki, Kailua, Hawaii

Item # 7301A

Awakening...To the Reality That You Are Never Alone

by Dr. Silke Vogelmann-Sine, Ph.D

Dr. Silke, a licensed psychologist with over 20 years of experience helping people to heal, introduces a new and astonishing view into our relationships with the higher vibrations of the non-physical self, stirring the emotions to new levels by creating a special safe space where one can begin to heal.

"Healing is a gift that we all share. I would like to share these guided meditations with optional journaling exercises to help you experience and explore your own personal connection to your innermost self, and create a new life filled with limitless possibilities for health, peace, joy and love."—Silke Vogelmann-Sine, Ph.D

Item # 43SV01

More Audiotapes from Kirael

The Wisdom of the Lost Scrolls

Kirael narrates a new series based on the ancient scrolls of the Alexandrian Library and presents insights that have never been revealed before.

Six 90-minute tapes each $9.95.

SPECIAL PRICE: Set of 5 for $39.95 -Item #7212

This series includes:

THE MYSTERY OF GENESIS

From the perspective of the Seventh Dimension, an amazing account of the beginnings of humankind on Earth. **Item #7212A**

THE MYSTERY OF REVELATION

An intriguing account about a channeled conversation with Master Jesus fifty years after his crucifixion. **Item #7212B**

THE LIFE OF JOHN THE BAPTIST

The awesome journey of the man who was "the Bridge" between the Old and New Testament. **Item #7212C**

THE AGENDAS OF PETER AND PAUL

Many historical questions are answered surrounding Peter, "The Rock," and Paul, "The Architect of Western Religion." **Item # 7212D**

THE LIFE AND TIMES OF MASTER JESUS

Kirael reveals many unknown facts of Jesus' journey and message of healing through Love. **Item #7212E**

THE LIFE AND TIMES OF MASTER JESUS

Kirael's astounding account of the conversations that took place between the 12 men and 12 women disciples the night before the crucifixion of Master Jesus. **Item #7212F**

Your Information Resource for the Great Shift

I.D.	Product Title	Price
7101	**Book:** Kirael: The Great Shift by Rev. Fred Sterling	$14.95
7102	**Book:** Kirael Vol. II: The Genesis Matrix by Rev Fred Sterling	$14.95
7301A	**CD:** The Power of Healing Prayers, Volume I by Kirael	$15.95
7302	**CD:** Unmask The Stranger by Band of Light	$15.95
7303	**CD:** Peace On Earth by Band of Light	$15.95
7401	**Video:** Kirael: The Messenger–VHS Format	$19.95
2401	**Video:** The Shift to Your Higher Self–VHS Format	$19.95
	90-minute Audiotapes by Kirael—in digital stereo:	
7200S	"An Evening with Kirael"—audio tape subscription/one year	$9.95
7201	Angels	$9.95
7202	Aspects, Splinters & Twin Flames	$9.95
7203	Christ Consciousness	$9.95
7204	The Female Energies that Surrounded Christ	$9.95
7205	The Galactic Brotherhood	$9.95
7206	The Great Shift	$9.95
7207	Photon Energy	$9.95
7208	Sharing Life With Your Ego	$9.95
7209	Signature Cell Healing	$9.95
7210	Time, Space—The Illusion	$9.95
7211	Transitioning Into the Light	$9.95
7212	Wisdom of the Lost Scrolls Series (6 audiotapes)	$47.95
7212A	The Mystery of Genesis	$9.95
7212B	The Mystery of Revelation	$9.95
7212C	The Life and Times of John the Baptist	$9.95
7212D	The Agendas of Peter and Paul	$9.95
7212E	The Life and Times of Master Jesus	$9.95
7212F	Conversations at the Last Supper	$9.95
7500S	Monthly "Kirael Shift Report" subscription for 1 year	$24.00
41DS01	**Book:** Radiant Light, Boundless Love by D. Shipman	$17.95
43SV01	**CD:** Awakening… To the Reality That You Are Never Alone	$24.00

***For further information on these great products,
Call toll-free 1-800-390-1886 or email: shopkirael@yahoo.com
Order on-line at www.inward.com***

The Honolulu Church of Light

A Healing Sanctuary

Led by Senior Minister and Director, Reverend Fred Sterling, Honolulu Church of Light was founded on the trinity of Truth, Trust, and Passion to create a space whereby all religious understandings are welcomed.

Our programs and services include:

- Sunday and Wednesday evening healing services
- Free Signature Cell Healing sessions, available by appointment
- Spiritual counseling services
- Prayer Services and Meditation Evenings
- Personal, Business or Community Blessings/Healings
- "Evenings with Kirael": monthly live transmedium sessions

Is there a wedding in your future?

The Honolulu Church of Light's spiritual wedding chapel is an oasis of light and love that will add the Hawaiian touch to your special day. Full-wedding packages are available at affordable rates.

"The Signature Cell Healing Experience" Workshops

Classes co-facilitated by Rev. Fred Sterling, pioneer of the Signature Cell Healing Technique, and a multi-disciplinary team of healers.

Please call the church for more information and registration.

Honolulu Church of Light
Call toll-free: 1-800-390-1886
Email: theshift@hula.net, Internet: www.inward.com